MW00885765

Help! I Think I've C
Unpardona
Why the Cross Makes ɪɪɪɪ impossible

Eddie Snipes

A book by:
Exchanged Life Discipleship

Copyright © 2017 by Eddie Snipes and
Exchanged Life Discipleship

http://www.exchangedlife.com

ISBN: 978-1544108179

Contact the author by visiting http://www.eddiesnipes.com or http://www.exchangedlife.com

Cover Photo Credit
© Can Stock Photo / bruesw

Table of Contents

Is Sin Greater than God?

Over nearly two decades in ministry, the most common question I'm asked is:

"Can you help me. I think I've committed the unpardonable sin."

This question has put many people in bondage, and because of many misconceptions being taught about this topic, it's a question that needs a clear, biblically based answer.

Rarely does a month go by when I don't hear someone ask this question. Sometimes it's several people a week. It's a reasonable question because many hear warnings about the unpardonable sin from books, TV, Bible classes, and even from the pulpit.

I also struggled with this fear prior to God's dramatic work in my life in early 1998. Growing up under hard-shell preaching, I often heard how a blasphemous thought, a willful sin, or even neglecting to do what is right could spell doom for my weakened soul. A few years back, when sharing my testimony, a man told me, "You can't be forgiven. The Bible says that if you fall away, you cannot be renewed again to repentance."

The verse he showed me was confusing, for I knew it wasn't the devil that turned my life around. So there had to be something wrong with how this verse was being used. This erroneous teaching made it more difficult for the younger me to overcome habitual sins, for it taught me to flee God, instead of coming to His throne of Grace for help in my time of need. I was afraid to come to God.

And herein is the evidence this teaching is not of God. According to the Bible, God's perfect love casts out all fear, and we are welcomed before Him when we need more grace. Let's stop for a moment and look at **1 John 4:16-19**

16 And we have known and believed the love that God has for us. God is love, and he who abides in love abides in God, and God in him.

¹⁷ Love has been perfected among us in this: that we may have boldness in the day of judgment; because as He is, so are we in this world.

¹⁸ There is no fear in love; but perfect love casts out fear, because fear involves torment. But he who fears has not been made perfect in love.

¹⁹ We love Him because He first loved us.

Fear is not the evidence that we are under condemnation; fear is the evidence that we don't understand the love of God. We are perfected by abiding in the love of God. Yet most people falsely believe that we must perfect our behavior before we can enter into the love of God.

Stop and meditate on verse 17 for a moment. You will be confident (or have boldness) in the day of judgment because we have been perfected by God's love. Keep in mind that the word for love is 'agape', which is the love of God given to us. Agape is never man's love toward God. Through the agape love of God, we enter into God's love, and through that fellowship, we are able to love God with the love we have first received from Him.

Now look at verse 16 again. How do you abide in God? By doing good deeds? By making changes in yourself? No. When you abide in God's love, you abide in God. When you focus on God's love, love perfects you. It's the work of God, but that work remains unrealized in your life until you trust in His love enough to receive it. It's not based on your worthiness, but it's based on the Lord's desire to reveal His love to you.

Love can only be fully understood when it is unconditional. When someone cannot earn love, that is when God reveals that His care for us is based on His nature, and not our abilities. The moment you try to earn, or try to become worthy of love, you are rejecting it to replace it with a bartering system. When you or I make God's love something we trade our good behavior to receive, we have devalued His love.

Your love for God is not dependent upon your ability to make yourself love Him. We love because we have first received love.

And because we know (which is our understanding of God's love) and believe (which is our faith in His love), we will have absolute confidence in judgment. The one thing everyone fears does not shake us, because we are in His love.

You should be so confident in God's love for you that nothing can shake you. Not even the unpardonable sin. We'll examine what the Bible specifically teaches about this topic later, but first you must believe in God's love. Without faith in the love He has revealed to you, confidence is impossible.

When I didn't understand this, I feared God's wrath and could not perceive His love. I once believed what religion taught me – that if I fell away, I could not be renewed with repentance. Because I had a habitual sin that I could not break, I failed to believe in God's grace (favor), and instead of letting God show Himself strong in my weakness, I tried to make myself strong for Him – which is impossible and fruitless.

Two decades ago, I had become so disillusioned by my inability to clean up my act, and the constant preaching of fear and condemnation, that I abandoned church completely. For nearly four years I lived for myself, allowing my sinful habit to rule my life. I stopped trying to overcome. Almost twenty years of efforts had accomplished nothing, and I felt more distant from God than ever before. Plus I kept hearing messages that warned me that if I didn't get my life right, I couldn't be right with God. All I heard was messages about judgment, condemnation, and wrath.

The beginning of the end of my church life started when I had a teacher give a lesson on Hebrews 10:26. He explained that if anyone falls away after receiving the knowledge of the truth, it is impossible to be renewed. "You better take care and not fall into sin. If you do, God will not receive you back," he said.

It was then that I realized that I could not measure up to God's perfect standard. As my hopelessness grew, I finally reached the point of giving up. Since my efforts were futile, why am I coming to hear my condemnation every week?

Years later, after God had miraculously revealed Himself to me, even though I abandoned the faith, I was back in the church with a new perspective and a confident hope. During one study, the opportunity came up and I shared my story.

After giving my testimony, I was again having this passage thrown at me. The very teaching that drove me out of the church was being used to rebut my testimony of God's amazing work in my life.

As I stated previously, a man confronted me. "You can't be forgiven." He opened to Hebrews and read the familiar passage. "You see? The Bible says that if you fall away, you can never again be renewed to repentance."

I waited while he surfed to a few other proof-texts. "You were a reprobate and a reprobate can never be forgiven," he insisted.

"You heard my testimony," I said. "I shared about a miraculous change and my deliverance. Who do you think did this? Satan would never set me free. This could only be the work of God."

"All I know is this," he patted his palm on his Bible, "According to MY Bible, you can't be forgiven."

This, of course, is completely false. The Bible does not say this, and I'll explain these passages shortly. When God first intervened in my life, I was both amazed and confused. How is it possible that God would pour His Spirit upon me and wash the habit I could not break away, if He was unwilling to pardon my sin again?

There had to be something wrong with the way this scripture was being used. In the next chapter, we'll rightly divide the word of truth, and you'll clearly see what that passage means, but for now, let's broaden our perspective.

In a conversation I had with a woman who was convinced she had blasphemed God in her thoughts and was now unforgiveable, I asked a question designed to make her stop and think. "Are you a better parent than God is?" I asked.

"What do you mean?" she asked.

She had a teenage daughter, so I asked her if her daughter had ever said anything negative about her that wasn't true. Of course she had. Most teenagers do. I went on to explain that the word blasphemy means to say something negative, revile against, or rail against God. So when her daughter accused her of being out to get her, being mean, or some of the other negative things frustrated teens say, that is blasphemy against a parent.

"Let me ask you another question," I said. "Did you declare that you will never forgive your daughter, cast her away from you, and disown her?"

"No," she said.

"Why not?"

"Because I love her no matter what," she said.

"Ah, I see. So if having a negative thought against God banishes you from Him forever, then not only are you a better parent than God, but your love is more powerful than God's. Either that, or something is wrong with what you've been taught about blasphemy against the Holy Spirit." I explained, "If God indeed cannot continue to love His children who sin or have a negative thought about Him, then the only options we have is to either declare that our love is stronger than His, or we need to seek a better understanding of these passages."

Do you see the irony of this erroneous teaching? Which is the greater form of blasphemy? To have a negative thought, or to declare God's love as so limited, that we can love our kids more than God is able to love us?

Which is the greater form of blasphemy? To expect forgiveness when we sin willfully, or to declare that our sins have more power than Christ? To declare ourselves or someone else as unforgivable is to say that the work of Christ can be destroyed by the sin of a person. It's to say that my sin is greater in power than the power of God to take away the sin of the world through His death on the cross, and the life-giving power of His resurrection.

In order for the Christian to be unpardonable, we must elevate the power of sin above Christ. To believe in the unpardonable sin is to create an idol we glorify as greater than God.

Keep in mind that the Bible says that the same Spirit that raised Jesus from the grave lives in you, and gives life to your mortal bodies, which is also the power to live in faith and overcome sin.

We'll also examine the willful sin next, but I want to look at how this false understanding limits many Christians, and limited me during my struggles. Since I knew I had sinned, and the teaching was that my sins drove a wedge between myself and God, I was afraid to seek help from the only source of strength given to the Christian. I had been taught that when I sinned, I had no right to come before God's throne until I first got my life right. Yet this is the complete opposite of what the Bible teaches. Look at **Hebrews 4:15-16**

> [15] For we do not have a High Priest who cannot sympathize with our weaknesses, but was in all *points* tempted as *we are, yet* without sin.
>
> [16] Let us therefore come boldly to the throne of grace, that we may obtain mercy and find grace to help in time of need.

Do you see a conflict between the doctrine of a Christian being separated from God, and this passage? You and I are *commanded* to come confidently (or boldly) before God's throne of grace for help when we are in need. The throne of grace is not limited to those who are thriving. It is especially for those who are struggling.

You don't need help in your time of need when you are sinless. Our need is for help when we are weak and failing. You already have grace, but when you are failing, God commands you to have enough trust in His grace to come to Him for *more* grace when you are in need. His grace is your help – and yes, that means when you have sinned. This is true, even if you have sinned repeatedly and can't seem to break free.

Here's a secret. You will never break free as long as you are trying to become righteous for God. God is your overcomer. His Spirit defeats man's weakness. What's better is that your weakness becomes God's strength. The Bible says to glory in your weakness, for when you are weak, the power of God rests upon you!

It wouldn't have taken me more than two decades to escape my sin if someone had taught me this early in my Christian life. The moment I cried out to the God I had abandoned with the words, "I can't do it. I can't live this Christian life. I can't defeat my sin," was the moment God's power rested upon me. That was the moment God said, "Now that you finally figured this out, let me show you what I can do." Then my sin died and my spiritual life came alive. When I learned to rest in faith, I was finally out of the way and allowing God to work.

With this being said, let me end this first chapter with a word of assurance. Even if you thought or said the most blasphemous idea possible for a man to declare, it cannot overthrow God's love for you. Nor can it defeat your life – unless you put your faith in sin, instead of in Christ.

There is no sin of thought, word, or deed that is powerful enough to separate you from the love of God or His plan of good for your life. Indeed, there are consequences to our actions, but even in defeat, God delights in unveiling His victory. There is not an unpardonable sin. Even some of the Pharisees that Jesus spoke this to came to faith after His resurrection. This was a warning that rejecting the Spirit's revelation of Christ blocked them from salvation, for there is hope in Christ alone. This will be clear when we examine these passages later.

For now, meditate on the truths that there is no fear in love. The one who abides in love abides in God. Those who know and believe in God's love will not have fear – even in the day of judgment.

God's love for you is greater than your weakness. He is greater than your sin. He is your Father, and a good father would never abandon his children. As Jesus said, "If you, being sinful, do good for your children, how *much more* will your heavenly Father, who is perfect, do good for you?"

It's time to stop trusting in words of condemnation, and start believing what God has said. It's time to stop trusting in sin, and start trusting in the power of God. It's time to lay your weaknesses at the throne of grace and receive His promise of strength. When you are weak, then you are strong, for the power of God rests upon you. Stop trying to be strong for God, and start being strong in God – which is allowing God to show Himself strong on your behalf.

Is Sin Greater than God?

God loves you more than you can comprehend. Rest in that truth and let God's love be lavished upon you! God's love is greater than your sins. No failure has the power to thwart the love of God. God's love is only limited by your unwillingness to believe enough to receive it.

Most of our struggles are the results of limiting God because we trust in the power of failure, problems, and our weaknesses more than we trust in His promise.

Rethinking Repentance

The word repent is translated from the Greek word, Metanoeo, which means to change the mind. It means to take our mind out of human thinking, and rest our minds in faith. Our minds need repentance, or a change of thinking, whether we are in temptation to sin, or the temptation of religion by human effort.

The majority of the scriptures that are used to condemn believers comes out of the Old Covenant of the Law. According to the scriptures, the law was designed to reveal the guilt of the entire world to show mankind we can never become righteous. Then through that condemnation, the law becomes our tutor, that leads us to Christ where all sin, condemnation, and guilt have been taken out of the way.[1]

This study will not be focusing on these passages, but on the misunderstood scriptures of the New Covenant. Let's first look at the often misused passage of **Romans 1:28**

> And even as they did not like to retain God in *their*
> knowledge, God gave them over to a debased mind, to do
> those things which are not fitting;

Some translations use 'reprobate' instead of 'debased'. After going down the lists of sins that mankind is caught up in, this passage is given to explain that God will indeed turn man over to the sins he is pursuing.

The problem comes when people use this as a prooftext that God writes people off forever. This passage is not saying that God gives up on man and turns him over to sin forever.

Because people are distracted by sin and its empty promises, sometimes people have to come to the end of themselves before they realize that there is no fulfillment in sin. The quickest way to discover that sin is a lie and cannot fulfill us or produce good is to allow it to fully run its course.

---

[1] Romans 3:19-24, Galatians 3:24-26

How many men have loved money and made obtaining it the obsession of their lives, only to look at what they have worked for and say, "Even with all these possessions, my life still has no meaning?"

What about the drug user that begins by pursuing the high? The moment of pleasure draws them in, but how many long-term drug users are happy? How many even like the drugs they use? They hate it, but it rules them with cravings and dependencies they cannot control or break away from.

How many youths have heard the warnings, but didn't believe until the drugs drove them to hopelessness? It isn't until their lives are turned upside down that they believe the warnings they ignored and now see it as a destructive force.

An illustration I like to use to explain this comes from my youth. I had a friend who thought it was cool to start smoking. He ignored his parent's warning and sneaked around to smoke. His father discovered this and confronted him. "So you want to smoke? Let's go to the store and buy you some cigarettes."

He bought a carton of the brand his son was using. They returned home and his dad took a coffee can, sat on the back porch and said, "Start smoking."

My friend's dad then told him he'd have to smoke the entire carton. Things went well until he finished smoke number six. He wanted to stop, but his dad laid down the law. "You are going to finish that entire carton. If you stop, I'm going to take my belt to your hide, and then you are going to come back to finish the carton."

His head spun as he finished the first pack. He was already feeling sick, but through his fog, his father's voice forced him to keep pressing forward. His dad was a big man and he didn't want to feel that belt. When he tried to slow down, the intimidating voice blasted him to press on.

He begged to stop. "I'm getting sick!"

"You will finish that carton!" his dad bellowed. He tried, but failed. A few more cigarettes and he collapsed on the porch. He was so sick, he couldn't get out of bed the rest of the day.

"From that day on, I could not stand the sight of a cigarette," he later said.

Was it cruel for his father to make him smoke until he was sick? No. My friend was looking at the temporal pleasure, but his father was looking at the long-term consequences. He loved his son enough to give temporal discomfort to change his child's mindset. If he punished him for smoking, the inner desire would still be there and he would continue to pursue the smoking. Instead, his father gave him over to what he thought he wanted and let the cigarettes convince him of their harm.

This is why God gives people over to their sins. He is not abandoning them, but allowing them to reach the point where sin is painful, so they see it's worthlessness. Then grace comes to reveal the true love of God. To force religious conformity will not change the heart.

The problem with legalistic Christianity is that it focuses on judgment and gives people the image of a God disdaining those who don't obey Him. Legalism attempts to force conformity, while the heart still believes that sin is better than God. It's as if God is denying us what is good, instead of teaching people what good really looks like. It tells people that sin is wrong, but is woefully lacking when it comes to unveiling the abundant life that flows out of grace, which flows out of God's love for you.

Romans 1 speaks about the sins that rule the lives of people, but that isn't the purpose of Romans 1. It is not designed to give the church a Christian club to thump sinners with. The purpose of Romans 1 is summarized in **Romans 2:1**

> Therefore you are inexcusable, O man, whoever you are who judge, for in whatever you judge another you condemn yourself; for you who judge practice the same things.

How quickly legalistic theology passes over this verse. You who judge are just as guilty. The next few verses warns us that we who judge will be judging ourselves and we are putting ourselves under the same judgement as those we are condemning.

So the purpose of this passage is not to create hopeless condemnation, but to set the stage to understand grace – namely that we are all in the same boat. The man who condemns adultery has lusted in his own heart, and according to Jesus, God doesn't see lusting as being any different than acting it out in the body. Romans chapters 1 through 3 lay out the sin problem in order to introduce the sin solution – grace through faith in Christ. By the law is the knowledge of sin, and the law condemns us all, but we escape the law through Christ, who fulfilled the law on our behalf.

If someone has told you that God turned you over to your sins, this only means that God is working to reveal to you that what has captured your desire is destructive, in order to help you see what good truly is.

There is another good illustration of this in 1 and 2 Corinthians. There was a man in the church living in a lifestyle so immoral that even the secular culture was appalled. The church turned the man over to Satan, which also means he was turned over to his sin. In 2 Corinthians, the Apostles instruct the church to restore this man to fellowship because he was in so much sorrow. He had come to the end of himself, and this drove him to turn his focus away from the sin he had once been addicted to.

This shows that God's ultimate goal is always restoration and spiritual health. The goal is not punishment, but restoration. God was not angry, but sorrowful over this man's destructive behavior.

Let's examine another passage – the dreaded unpardonable verse. **Hebrews 10:26-27**

> ^{26} For if we sin willfully after we have received the knowledge of the truth, there no longer remains a sacrifice for sins,
> ^{27} but a certain fearful expectation of judgment, and fiery indignation which will devour the adversaries.

When read out of context, this causes most people to feel hopeless, for who hasn't sinned willfully? For most of my Christian life, this passage troubled me. I asked dozens of people to explain this, and got many, many answers. The most common was that God cannot forgive willful sins.

The problem with this idea is all sin is willful. Sin occurs when we believe we know what God wants us to do, or not to do, but choose our will over God's. By default, sin is when our will is contrary to God's, and we decide to follow ours. All sin is willful. We find creative ways to make our conscious feel it isn't rebellion, but at the heart of all sin is a will that is in contradiction with God's.

However, this passage is not speaking about our individual sins. Part of the problem is that the Bible was not written in chapters and verses. Over the years, theologians have divided the Bible up to make it easier to navigate, but the division of a verse does not mean it's a separate thought or subject to the rest of the book of the Bible.

The context of a passage is critical. We should always ask ourselves what is the complete thought being communicated. Then, how does that fit into the broader subject of the chapter or book of the Bible. Then how does that fit into the covenant we are studying (New or Old), then how does it fit into the Bible as a whole. This is what the Bible calls, "Rightly dividing the word of truth."

The book of Hebrews was written to Jewish Christians. Jews are called Hebrews, hence the name of the book. The book of Hebrews is written to a Jewish church under intense pressure and persecution for breaking away from the Old Covenant. Under the New Covenant, we have a new priest, Jesus. The old sacrificial system passed away because Jesus was the final sacrifice, and the old temple worship was changed when God declared that he now inhabits the heart of the believer. According to the Bible, you are the temple of God. It is no longer a building.

Because of outside pressure, many Jewish Christians were compromising their faith and trying to add the Old Covenant law into their worship.

When you read the entire book of Hebrews, you will see it is a systematic explanation of how the law pointed to Christ and was a shadow, and not the real thing. When the real thing came (Jesus) the shadows that pointed to Him were taken away. To go back to the things that foreshadowed Christ was to deny Christ.

Hebrews then compares the shadows to the real thing. It compares the priesthood to Christ and affirms that Jesus is now our ONLY High Priest. It compares the animal sacrifices to Christ to show that it was insufficient, and the old system only pointed to the coming sacrifice of the body of Christ on the cross. The temple worship was replaced by Christ as well.

The key to understanding Hebrews 10:26 is **Hebrews 10:1-5**

[1] For the law, having a shadow of the good things to come, *and* not the very image of the things, can never with these same sacrifices, which they offer continually year by year, make those who approach perfect.

[2] For then would they not have ceased to be offered? For the worshipers, once purified, would have had no more consciousness of sins.

[3] But in those *sacrifices there is* a reminder of sins every year.

[4] For *it is* not possible that the blood of bulls and goats could take away sins.

[5] Therefore, when He came into the world, He said: "Sacrifice and offering You did not desire, But a body You have prepared for Me.

Since the blood of the animal sacrifices could never take away sin, those who willfully turn back to that system of worship do not find a cleansed conscience, but instead have a fearful expectation of judgment. Why does the old system only create fear of judgment? Because the blood of the animal can NEVER take away sin. Only Christ can do this. So if the Jewish Christians turned from the knowledge of the truth of Christ, and back to a system that can't remove sin, they find guilt instead of freedom.

Even then, it's not a condemnation of eternal judgement. All they need to do is leave the dead works of the law behind, and put their trust in Christ. There is no more sacrifice for sin because Jesus is the final sacrifice. This passage is a call to turn from the law, and back to Christ. This doesn't even apply to the non-Jewish Christians – unless you are one of those who have been convinced to bring the law and its ordinances into the church.

A passage that was designed to give us confidence in Christ alone has been misapplied. Instead of the intended purpose to explain why Christ took us out of the law, it is now being misapplied to our behavior, and causes many to live under the greater sin, disbelieving that Jesus is sufficient to take away all sin.

I can't leave this topic without mentioning Jesus' interactions with the Pharisees. **Matthew 12:31-32**

> 31 "Therefore I say to you, every sin and blasphemy will be forgiven men, but the blasphemy *against* the Spirit will not be forgiven men.
> 32 "Anyone who speaks a word against the Son of Man, it will be forgiven him; but whoever speaks against the Holy Spirit, it will not be forgiven him, either in this age or in the *age* to come.

Once again, this was not directed at the Christian, but at those who were rejecting Christ and trying to prevent others from believing.

The Pharisees were students of the Old Testament. Jesus began his ministry by quoting from Isaiah by saying, "The Spirit of the LORD is upon Me, Because He has anointed Me To preach the gospel to the poor; He has sent Me to heal the brokenhearted, To proclaim liberty to the captives And recovery of sight to the blind, To set at liberty those who are oppressed; To proclaim the acceptable year of the LORD"

The anointing is a reference to Jesus being anointed by the Spirit at His baptism. Because Jesus veiled His glory, everything Jesus did was through the power of the Holy Spirit – the same Spirit you and I received.

The Pharisees saw the works that were foretold in the very scriptures they were experts in knowing. They saw the prophecies being fulfilled before their eyes. They even plotted to kill Lazarus, the man Jesus raised from the dead, in order to hide the work of the Spirit. The power of the Spirit is being plainly shown before their eyes, and God is revealing the gift of salvation to them, but they trusted in their own religious activities, and hated Christ and the Spirit working through the miracles He did.

They called the work of the Spirit the acts of the Devil. They were rejecting the only thing that could bring salvation, so they cannot be forgiven. Keep in mind that it is the Spirit that draws people to Christ, so if someone rejects the Spirit, they cannot be transformed into the new creation God designed for each person when they enter Christ.

This does not apply to you. You cannot think a thought blasphemous enough to offend the Spirit. God cannot reject Himself, so you cannot be rejected by God. Let's conclude with this passage from **2 Timothy 2:13**

If we are faithless, He remains faithful; He cannot deny Himself.

If you are born of God, His Spirit is within you, He placed a new spirit within you (which is your new life), and that Spirit is the seed of God, according to the Bible. Eternal life cannot be extinguished, any more than God can be extinguished. The blasphemy of the Holy Spirit only applied to those who were rejecting Christ and calling the Holy Spirit the devil. Those who receive the Spirit cannot blaspheme – even if they have a bad thought against God. This does not apply to you.

It's also ironic that Jesus said this applied to those who were rejecting the revelation of Christ and SPEAKING against the Spirit. Religion has taken a warning about unbelieving Pharisees speaking, and turned it into a warning against believers THINKING. No passage says anyone is condemned for a blasphemous thought. This is typical of religion. It takes laws and creates more laws. Legalism seeks more ways to condemn, yet Jesus said that He came to set the oppressed free, and proclaim the acceptance of God to you, through Christ.

Fear creates thoughts of condemnation. In the next chapter, we'll look at why bad thoughts trouble us, and how we can bring every thought captive.

Rethink the Way You Think

Why do bad thoughts enter our minds? Why is it so hard to get our minds out of negative ways of thinking? Many years ago, I was speaking with a man who was tormented with uncontrollable thoughts about God's anger.

"I try to make myself stop thinking these blasphemous thoughts, but it keeps coming into my head. No matter how hard I try, I can't stop it, even though I hate thinking this way," he said.

It began with a sermon he heard about God's wrath. The sermon focused on blaspheming the Holy Spirit, and the preacher warned the audience that if they even thought blasphemy against the Holy Spirit, their souls would be doomed.

This is when his problem began. He worried that he might do this, and sure enough, a thought popped in. He stressed out about it, confessed his sin to God, but the thoughts kept coming. By the time he spoke to me, he was convinced he was destined for hell, and his thoughts were continually on blasphemous things.

As we have seen in the previous chapter, this doctrine comes from misapplied scriptures. If that wasn't bad enough, these erroneous doctrines have taken the warning of the Pharisees speaking against the work of the Spirit, and it has morphed into condemnation for a thought.

Jesus never said that a bad thought would condemn you to hell. In fact, the focus of His comments to the Pharisees was based on these religious leaders using their influence to turn people away from God. He said, "Woe to you...You did not enter yourselves, and those who were entering, you hindered." This is what made the blasphemy so great. It wasn't merely their rejection, but that they were trying to keep people from responding to the call of the Spirit. And somehow we have turned the gospel of peace into the gospel of fear, putting believers under condemnation for even having a bad thought.

So why do blasphemous thoughts enter our heads? And why do people try to stop thinking something, only to have thoughts become worse and often to the point of overflooding their minds?

For the most part, the answer is fear. Let's take the example of the man who heard the message with the warning of judgment if he had a blasphemous thought. His struggles began with fear of thinking something, and sure enough, he started thinking of the very thing he was trying to avoid. Why is this?

Let us take a moment to step into the world of psychology. Some people are opposed to psychology in Christianity, but it's merely the study of how the mind works.

God has designed the mind as an amazing and complex system, that if healthy, gives us intelligence, creativity, problem solving skills, and a healthy emotional balance. Our minds have also been designed with conscious and subconscious thought.

If you didn't have a subconscious thought system, everything would need to be your focus, and resolving issues would be nearly impossible. I like to call the subconscious 'your researcher'. He carries the load to resolve issues you present as problems. Let me give an example.

A few years back I led an IT team that was called to resolve a problem. There was a network issue that a company was having trouble resolving. We checked all the usual configurations and hardware, but the problem was something out of the ordinary. I spent many hours working out the problem and trying solutions. I did everything I could think of, but couldn't find the root of the issue. Late in the evening, we decided to break for the night and start again in the morning. My mind was exhausted, so I decided to not think about the issue until the next day.

I had an hour drive home, so I decided to listen to music and relax my brain. Forty-five minutes into my commute, my researcher tossed an idea into my conscious thought. "What do you think about this?" In a moment of inspiration, I had the answer to the problem. Sure enough, the next morning I applied this solution, and the problem was resolved in a few short minutes.

How does that happen? I wasn't trying to resolve the problem at that moment, but my subconscious researcher took what I had been focused on, and worked on a solution in the background. When he found a good prospect, he tossed the potential solution into my mind.

What an amazing gift of God our minds are! What a wonderful design to give us a brain that can work while we are at rest. During the time we are focused on something, we're feeding our subconscious information that it will take, process, and present solutions beyond what we thought possible.

The great inventor, Nikola Tesla, was thinking of a way to turn direct current electricity into a more manageable solution. DC poses many problems and risks for long distance connectivity. One day, Tesla was walking down the road and an amazing idea popped into his head. He built the first AC generator from a moment of inspiration, and it worked on his first design. The era of home electricity came to be out of a thought popping into his head. His researcher took what he focused on, worked out the details, and presented a solution that impacted the world.

So what happens if what we focus on is harmful or destructive? In the IT world, we have a term called 'Garbage in, Garbage out.' What you put in is what you will get out.

Let's go back to the sermon on blasphemy. The man hearing that sermon started focusing on blasphemous ideas. He focused on fear. He sent his researcher to work on what he was afraid of.

A behavioral researcher named Robert Maurer made an interesting observation as he studied many people. He said that your subconscious mind doesn't have the ability to discern a good question from a bad question. If you ask yourself a question more than three times, your mind will work on an answer. So if you say, "Why am I so stupid," your researcher will work on finding you the answer. What do you think will happen if you keep asking yourself about blasphemy?

What was the guy asking himself after hearing the sermon on blasphemy? "Have I ever had a blasphemous thought?" Because he added fear into the mix, his researcher doubled down on finding the answer. When his researcher found a qualifying thought, he introduced it. "Does this qualify as blasphemy against the Holy Spirit."

"Oh, no!" he lamented. Through fear, he focused more mental resources on that thought, showing his researcher that it was an important problem, so his subconscious continued focusing on it. A system of problem resolution that God designed to help us resolve life's problems was now out of control. It wasn't the subconscious that was out of control, but how he perceived God and his own thoughts.

What would happen if a blasphemous thought popped into his head, and he just shrugged it off? Do you think his subconscious would continue to work on that problem? No. He would have told his researcher, "This is not important."

When my daughter was eight, she hated skeletons. They creeped her out. I hated driving by decorated houses during Halloween, because skeletons abound.

Since she hated them so much, what do you think she thought about when she laid down? Periodically, she would go through a phase where our nightly routine was helping her not to be afraid to go to sleep.

One day, after several nights of being called into her room, I took a different approach. She called me, "Daddy, when I close my eyes, I see an ugly skeleton," she said.

I entered the room and told her we were going to do something different. "Close your eyes," I said. "Now I want you to see the skeleton."

"I don't like it," she said.

"I know, but let's do something new." I had her close her eyes and view the skeleton, then I said, "Now I want you to put a wig on him. Make the goofiest wig you can think of." Then we put a tutu on him, makeup, and did as many silly things as I could think of. She giggled, and her sister wanted to decorate a skeleton, too. They giggled while we desecrated the skeleton with girlie things, then she went right to sleep.

The next day, she called me again, and we went through the same process. This happened three or four days in a row, and I never heard my daughter mention a skeleton again. From age four to eight, it was a never-ending issue. From eight to adult, it was gone forever.

Once the fear was gone, she was no longer alerting her researcher to focus on this problem. Then her mind went on to more healthy and creative things.

This is why the previous chapter was built on eliminating the fear of blasphemy. God never intended for you to be afraid of offending Him. Look up fear in the New Testament. How many times does God tell us not to fear, not to be afraid, and even assures us that we will not even have fear on the Day of Judgement? Perfect love casts out all fear. When you hear a message of condemnation, does that build you up in the assurance of God's love, or does it create fear?

What creates a healthy spiritual life, being afraid of God, or being assured that He loves you without conditions? Which message is based on truth, one that makes people dread God's easily offended ego, or one that teaches people to rest in His love?

The Bible tells us that love (agape) covers a multitude of sins. Love casts out fear. We are even assured that love produces the fruit of the Spirit. The fruit of the spirit is love, and out of love comes joy, peace, longsuffering, kindness, goodness, faith, gentleness, self-control.

The English translations don't make this clear. It is listed as love being in the same list as the other evidences of the Spirit, but the proper way to translate this from the original Greek would be, "The fruit of the Spirit is love: joy, peace, patience..." The fruit of the Spirit is love, and from love we have joy, peace, and all the other attributes that indicate spiritual health.

Are you lacking in joy, or peace? Then you need to let the Spirit fill you with the love of God. Are you struggling with a sinful habit? Then you need to focus on abiding in God's love, and let His Spirit produce self-control. The Bible says that if you abide in God's agape love, you abide in God.

Many teach this backwards by saying, "If you stop sinning, God will love you." The Bible teaches that if you learn to abide in love, God's Spirit of love will work in you to produce self-control, which will naturally bring an end to sin. Your struggles are the evidence that you don't understand how to receive God's love. It goes against human ways of thinking, so we all struggle to be loved. If people get mad, they withdraw love as a punishment. That's because man is not love. People can show love, but they do not have a nature based on perfect love.

The Bible tells us, "God is love." Man's love is called 'philia' in the Greek. That word means friendship or warm affection. It is a response type of love. It is limited by human abilities and is often conditional. Actually, it's always conditional, but sometimes it's hard to break the conditions. My kids are mine, and I love them no matter what. It's still based on selfish motives, because they are mine. I love other children, but those conditions are much more limited than the conditions for my own children. It's hard to stop thinking of kids as belonging to us, so that love is hard to break. Most other philia love is very conditional. Couples divorce, friends have rifts, people offend or even try to harm us, and these things break down philia love.

Agape is not so. Agape is the love of God. God is agape, and if you read 1 Corinthians 13:4-13, you'll find a good definition of agape love. According to the Bible, the Spirit pours agape into our heart. Until then, we only have human love. But God's love is not conditional upon human performance. Love (agape) does not seek its own. It keeps no records of wrong. It is not provoked. It thinks no evil.

God's love for you is not demanding, but supplying. God gives without conditions. If you disobey, God does not withdraw love. If you act selfishly, God does not stop loving you. In fact, there is nothing you can do to make God love you more than He already does. Nor is there anything you can do to make God love you less.

The only limitation to agape love is your willingness to receive it. Temptation calls us to trust in the love of the world, but that doesn't mean that God no longer loves. It means that we are facing the wrong direction. The Bible says, "If anyone loves the world, the love of the Father is not in him."[2] It does not say that the limitation is on God's love, but rather or ability to receive and abide in it. Love is not withdrawn; it is pushed aside by us for something lesser.

Fear and condemnation do not limit God's love; it limits our belief in that love. If I believe God is seething with rage, then I hide from His love, believing that I am hiding from his rage. The same is true for condemnation. It causes us to look down in shame, instead of up with expectation.

God is not angry at your blasphemous thoughts. God's deep love has compassion on you during the time of need, and He wants to rescue you from being ruled by your thoughts. The same is true for lustful thoughts, anger, envy, hatred, fear, self-loathing, and any other plague of the mind. God even wants to rescue you from destructive religious thinking.

When you are at your worst, God is looking on you with compassion as His child that He desires to build up. God will never call you worthless, evil, or any negative thing. He will only call you child and friend. In fact, the only difference between a child and a friend is the level of maturity.

A child has to be guided and built up into understanding. But a mature child soon becomes a friend of the parent. My parents don't try to direct my life anymore. That child-parent relationship matured into friendship as I became an adult. As you mature in the love of God, you'll discover a companionship with God that is greater than any other friendship. God has invited us into the companionship between the Father, Son, and Spirit. It is a deep understanding of His love that perfects us into maturity.

In Jesus' prayer in John 17:23, He explained that the Father loves us just as He loves Jesus. How much is Jesus loved? You are just as loved. If you aren't experiencing this, something is preventing you from seeing it. But when you know and believe in the love He has for you, His perfect love casts out all fear, and it will produce in your life the evidence of love: joy, peace, patience, goodness, kindness, and self-control. Instead of having to force

---

[2] 1 John 2:15

yourself to do these things, the working of love will naturally produce these things. Sin dies because it is forced out of our lives by the agape love of God.

It's not your responsibility to do the work of the Spirit. Rest in love and let the Spirit perfect you. Don't allow fear, condemnation, or your own weaknesses or failures to persuade you to stop believing in God's love for you. It gives God pleasure when you allow Him to love you without conditions. God does not limit his love for you through religious conditions, nor unbelief, and certainly not sins or failures. When you believe in His love, you will trust Him with your sins. That's when miracles begin.

In the next chapter, we'll discuss the scriptures that guide us into healthy ways of thinking.

Reprogramming Your Thinker

2 Timothy 1:7

> For God has not given us a spirit of fear, but of power and of love and of a sound mind.

If God hasn't given us a spirit of fear, then why do so many belief systems associate God with anger, condemnation, and the threat of judgment? As discussed in a previous chapter, part of the problem stems from the confusion of mixing the Old and New Covenants.

The Old Covenant was designed to prove to mankind that goodness only comes from God. Twice in biblical history, man substituted God's righteousness for human effort. Adam rejected the goodness of God to pursue the temptation of the serpent, who said, "You can know good and evil." Adam stepped away from the tree of life, where everything was a gift of God, to take hold of the fruit of the knowledge of good and evil, to attempt to make himself the source of good through works.

Likewise, when God took His people out of the captivity of Egypt and led them to safety, He required nothing but faith. But the people were focused on human effort. The people called out for the law by saying, "We will do all that is commanded." They trusted in their obedience as the source of good.

When man tries to make himself an equal to God, the Lord invites him to do so. If you want to be perfectly acceptable to God, here is what good looks like. Give it your best shot. However, when mankind makes himself the source of good, the standard that measures good will be applied. The law is the straight stick of righteousness that is laid beside man to reveal whether he measures up. The law does not make man good. The law is the litmus test that says, are you perfect, or do you fall short?

This is why the Bible calls the law our tutor (or school master) that brings us to Christ. It teaches man that he is not the source of good, and then points to Christ. Once it delivers us to Christ, the law relinquishes its role. Consider **Romans 10:4**

> For Christ *is* the end of the law for righteousness to everyone who believes.

Jesus also alluded to this when He said, "Do not think I came to destroy the law, but to fulfill it."[3] Once He fulfilled it, Jesus took the penalty of the law that was due us, and took it upon Himself. That is why the Bible says in **2 Corinthians 5:21**

> For He made Him who knew no sin *to be* sin for us, that we might become the righteousness of God in Him.

You are not righteous because of what you do. You are righteous because God has given you His righteousness as a gift of His love, and as an act of love, He also took your sin upon Himself. You are the righteousness OF God. You are not producing your righteousness FOR God.

Do you understand that when you try to become righteous, you are pushing aside the righteousness of God? You are attempting to replace the perfection of God with your own personal efforts. It is a rejection of the completed work of Christ and the gift of righteousness when you try to make yourself acceptable to God.

Do you also realize that when you focus on your sin, you are snubbing the work of Christ? When you receive condemnation, you are rejecting the gift of righteousness through disbelief. How righteous is God? Can you do better than God's righteousness? If the answer is 'no', then what are you striving for? You already have the highest form of righteousness possible. You are the righteousness of God! Don't deny God's gift by claiming to be a sinner, which God has already said was placed upon Christ.

God has given you the great exchange. Don't swap back. If you have been taught like most of us, your belief system has been centered around you, instead of Christ. That's okay. Now is the day to trust in what Jesus called, "The acceptable day of the Lord." Turn

---

[3] Matthew 5:17

your mind to faith, and start receiving grace instead of condemnation and fear!

Fear can only exist where love is shunned. We shun God's love because we don't feel worthy, yet the point of the law was to show us that we can never be worthy. Man, at his best, falls short. Not one person succeeded under the law. What little success you find in the Old Testament is God showing mercy to those who trusted in Him. It was never based on what someone accomplished for God.

We often hear about the Fear of the Lord. We are taught that we should be afraid of God's harsh hand if we do wrong, but is that really what the fear of the Lord is about? It is not. Let me show two passages that make this clear.

Isaiah 53 is the great messianic prophecy that foretells of Jesus' sacrifice for our sins. It tells that our savior will be bruised for our transgressions and our sins will be laid upon Him.

Isaiah 54 speaks of the results of Jesus' work. Because Jesus took away our sin, we have the promise of **Isaiah 54:8-10**

8 With a little wrath I hid My face from you for a moment; But with everlasting kindness I will have mercy on you," Says the LORD, your Redeemer.

9 "For this *is* like the waters of Noah to Me; For as I have sworn That the waters of Noah would no longer cover the earth, So have I sworn That I would not be angry with you, nor rebuke you.

10 For the mountains shall depart And the hills be removed, But My kindness shall not depart from you, Nor shall My covenant of peace be removed," Says the LORD, who has mercy on you.

Just as Isaiah 53 was fulfilled at the cross, we are now in the promise of Isaiah 54. Under the law, God hid His face for a moment, but through Christ, we have His everlasting kindness and the promise that wrath cannot be revived. Notice the strength of the promise. God has sworn by His own name that He cannot be angry at you and His wrath CANNOT return. It's not based on you. This promise is based on God's covenant with Himself. He has sworn an oath that cannot be removed.

Your sin cannot defeat the work of Christ. Your failures cannot cause God to return to wrath. Wrath is off the table. Once you receive Christ, you can never again be under God's wrath. If there is anything in God's word you believe, believe this. God could not have said it any clearer. This is for you!

Since this is an unshakeable truth, what is the fear of the Lord? How can we fear the Lord, without being in fear? It's one of the great paradoxes of scripture. A clear piece of this picture can be found in **Jeremiah 32:38-40**

> [38] `They shall be My people, and I will be their God;
> [39] `then I will give them one heart and one way, that they may fear Me forever, for the good of them and their children after them.
> [40] `And I will make an everlasting covenant with them, that I will not turn away from doing them good; but I will put My fear in their hearts so that they will not depart from Me.

There is more to this promise, but before we look at it, let me draw your attention to the one doing the action. Who changes the heart? God said, "I will give them one heart and one way. I will make an everlasting covenant. I will put my fear in their hearts so they will not depart."

This isn't your responsibility. Your only responsibility is to look at Christ and trust in His completed work. Your only role is to receive the gift of faith, and through faith you learn to trust in God's love for you and works for you. Even faith is not your responsibility. The Bible says that God deals each person a measure of faith, and that the Spirit gives us more faith as a gift of the Spirit. Not refusing is your only role. But let's go on. Look now at **Jeremiah 33:9**

> `Then it shall be to Me a name of joy, a praise, and an honor before all nations of the earth, who shall hear all the good that I do to them; they shall fear and tremble for all the goodness and all the prosperity that I provide for it.'

How have we gotten so far off course in the church? It is the recognition of God's goodness that causes people to fear. It's not fear of wrath, but the overwhelming recognition of God's goodness. The world cannot understand grace, so they fear what they don't understand.

Praise is born in the heart that sees how much God is expressing His love toward them. You are in the ground shaking acts of God's love, and those who see God's work in you shall fear. Are people trembling with amazement of God's love for the church? Or are they given the false version of worldly fear that God hates them?

When you start experiencing God's love, that is when you are a true witness for God. But in order to experience the fullness of your life in the Spirit, you must stop thinking like someone of the flesh. The Bible promises you that if you walk in the Spirit, you will not fulfill the lusts of the flesh. This goes hand-in-hand with the promise that as you behold the glory of Christ, you are transformed into that same glory by the power of the Spirit working in you.

You are already an overcomer. You are already more than a conqueror. The only thing that prevents you from walking in this is your mind stuck in the flesh. Thankfully, the Bible gives us the tools to reprogram our ways of thinking. Let's take a moment to examine how to gain control of our thought life. Start with **2 Corinthians 10:4-5**

> [4] For the weapons of our warfare *are* not carnal but mighty in God for pulling down strongholds,
> [5] casting down arguments and every high thing that exalts itself against the knowledge of God, bringing every thought into captivity to the obedience of Christ,

Here is our first change of thinking. You can't defeat the flesh and negative ways of thinking by trying to force your mind under your control. It's not human effort. It's surrender. Your weapons against the world (including your own flesh) is not carnal. Carnal means fleshly, or by human effort. Your might is in God. He pulls down all strongholds when we trust Him enough to rest in His promises.

Every thought is taken captive by surrendering them to the obedience OF CHRIST. It's not your obedience that's in charge here. Jesus' obedience is credited to you, and when you have struggles, you simply trust them into Christ's hands. You don't need to worry about getting your life right. Your life is right the moment you are looking to Christ.

When a thought troubles you, let go of it and trust Christ to bring it into captivity through His work of obedience. When you find yourself overtaken by sin or a sinful habit, release it into Jesus' hands. Put your trust in Him and claim the promise that God will cause you to walk in His ways. This is reiterated in **Micah 7:19**

He will again have compassion on us, And will subdue our iniquities. You will cast all our sins Into the depths of the sea.

This is no longer a 'He will'. Now that the New Covenant of Christ has been established, this passage is now 'He has.' Not only has God cast all your sin into the depths of the sea, but you are also under the promise that God "will subdue your iniquities." It's God's job to suppress sin in your life. It's God's job to subdue your thoughts. It's God's job to take every thought captive to the obedience of Christ. It's your job to trust Him and allow God to work in you.

Fear drives people to distrust God because they expect anger and judgment, when God has promised compassion and to work for our good. The Bible speaks against fear. Instead it instructs us to rest in His love. Consider the commands and promises of **Philippians 4:6-8**

^{6} Be anxious for nothing, but in everything by prayer and supplication, with thanksgiving, let your requests be made known to God;
^{7} and the peace of God, which surpasses all understanding, will guard your hearts and minds through Christ Jesus.
^{8} Finally, brethren, whatever things are true, whatever things *are* noble, whatever things *are* just, whatever things

are pure, whatever things *are* lovely, whatever things *are* of good report, if *there is* any virtue and if *there is* anything praiseworthy-- meditate on these things.

The command is to be anxious for nothing. The next time fear or bad thoughts plague you, give thanks, surrender it in prayer, and rest in God's promises. Then you are receiving the promise that God will guard your heart and mind through Christ.

Since God knows our minds can't operate in a vacuum, He has told us what to set our minds on as we release the negative things to Him. Meditate on these things. Everything here is praiseworthy and good.

When you try to do this, negative thoughts will pop up again. Remember, your researcher is still working on what he thinks is important to you. It's the things that once ruled your mind. When those thoughts pop up, remember to be anxious for nothing. It's not a big deal. Release the new thought to Christ. When that blasphemous, lustful, angry, or envious thought pops up, just say, "I think this belongs to you," and give it to Jesus. Then put your mind on praiseworthy things. You can start with thanking God that this thought cannot harm you. Thank God for putting tutus on your skeletons and disarming fear.

Sometimes that is exactly what you may have to do. When a thought won't stop troubling you, take that thought to Christ and imagine Him transforming it into something harmless. Instead of hiding in fear, take that blasphemous thought and imagine Jesus replacing everything negative with something positive. As you disarm the fear factor, your mind will stop treating these thoughts as something important and it will fade away.

Be anxious for nothing. Since God isn't angry, you should not fret. Release to Christ and let the fear of your thoughts be disarm. Instead of using your creativity to imagine fret and worry, use it to transform your mind by meditating on praiseworthy things.

Finally, let's conclude this chapter with **Romans 12:2**

And do not be conformed to this world, but be transformed by the renewing of your mind, that you may prove what *is* that good and acceptable and perfect will of God.

There is a saying, "Any dead fish can float downstream." To be conformed to this world, just let yourself go. The renewing of the mind is a course correction. As the world pulls us away, we are re-centered on Christ as we renew our mind. We do this through the word, through prayer, and through meditating on the things of the Spirit.

Don't allow anyone to condemn you, when God has declared you as free from the law and condemnation. Don't allow your mind to be conformed to fear by listening to any teaching that denies the basic principles of what God has declared:

He has sworn that He cannot be angry with you.

There is therefore no condemnation to those in Christ.

God is love.

Perfect love casts out all fear.

God suppresses sin.

It's the Spirit's job to transform you.

Hearing the word produces faith.

Since faith comes by hearing the word of God, any message that does not draw you to trust God more is a misuse of scripture, and isn't the word of truth. Rest in Christ. Rest in assurance. Transform your mind through the word.

Reprogramming Your Thinker

Rethinking Bondage

John 8:34

> Jesus answered them, "Most assuredly, I say to you, whoever commits sin is a slave of sin."

It's commonly taught that each time you sin, you are back under bondage to sin. This passage seems to affirm this, but it's also a good example of why context is so important.

By itself, this passage can be misunderstood, but in context, Jesus is pointing to the truth of Himself as our savior from sin. He tells the people, "If you abide in My word, you shall know the truth and it will make you free."

The Pharisees scoffed at this idea and declared that they were not in bondage to anyone. That is when Jesus warns them that anyone who has committed a sin is sin's slave, but then declares, "Whom the Son set's free is free indeed."

In other words, when Jesus sets you free, it is not a temporary fix, but you are indeed free. He even explains that the slave of sin does not abide forever, but those adopted as sons will remain forever. To understand this, we must understand what slavery to sin means, how we are redeemed out of slavery, and why we cannot fall from sonship back into bondage.

Let me first point out an important truth. There is the noun of sin, and the verb of sin. The noun of sin was eliminated. When Jesus began His ministry, the Bible calls Him, "The Lamb of God who takes away the sin of the whole world." The noun of sin, which is our prison and master, was defeated on the cross.

Someone in the prison of sin doesn't become free because they do a good deed. Those in the prison of sin are sinners, and a sinner does not become righteous because they do a righteous act. The verb (or act) of righteous deeds does not transform a sinner into a non-sinner. They are in the prison of sin, and no matter how many good deeds they do, they are still a slave of sin.

A son of God has become the righteousness of God, and they are in the house of righteousness. They have left the prison of slavery and are now bound to God's righteousness. An act of sin does not make those in righteousness sinners, just as an act of good does not make sinners righteous. Jesus defeated the noun of sin, and He set the captives of sin free. Those whom the Son sets free are free indeed.

To understand this, we need to go back and look at the word picture of slavery in the Bible. In our western culture, we think of slavery in light of the 1700s and 1800s, where people were taken against their will and forced into slavery. This practice is strictly forbidden in the Bible. (See 1 Timothy 1:10).

The slavery spoken of in the Bible is a legal contract. When someone borrowed money in the ancient world, there was no such thing as bankruptcy. There had to be collateral. People had to put up their land as collateral. If someone did not have land, they put themselves up as collateral. If they were borrowing enough money, they might put up their family as collateral.

If the debt could not be paid, they had to pay back the debt with service as a slave. Generally speaking, slavery would be measured based on the daily wage of that era. They and their family would have to go into slavery until the set number of days or years were fulfilled. Sometimes it could be the remainder of their lives, if it were enough money. Even death could not wipe out the debt against a family. You see a picture of this in 2 Kings 4. The father of the family had died, and the creditors were coming to take his sons into slavery, and the prophet Elisha used the miracle of the oil so His widow could sell enough to pay off the debt.

Once someone was in debt and could not pay, their only option was slavery. Slavery was the rightful payment of the debt, and in the book of Philemon, you see the Apostle Paul sending the slave, Onesimus, back to his master with a letter asking for leniency. The reason Paul sent him back was because he borrowed money and owed service to repay what he rightfully owed. Philemon made the decision to set the slave free so he could serve in ministry with Paul.

The Bible uses the Old Testament law of slavery as an amazing picture of the work of Christ. Once someone was in slavery, the owner did not have to accept payment. If a friend chose to loan the money (which would be rare), the slave master did not have to set them free. It might be more profitable to keep the slave instead of taking the money. But there was an exception in the law – the law of the Kinsman Redeemer.

If a kinsman (or close relative) came to make a rightful claim over the slave, he could pay the debt on behalf of his relative, and the owner had to set the slave free. This is why Jesus is called, our Redeemer. This law was a foreshadow of God adopting us as His child, and our kinsman, Christ, paying off our debt.

Let's digress for a moment to explore why understanding biblical slavery is a powerful truth that applies to our Christian life.

A slave has limited rights. The Bible gives the indebted slave some protection, but a slave can't own property, can't earn money, and can't enter into any legal agreements. A slave can never earn his own way out of slavery because anything he earns rightfully belongs to his master. Whether he works hard, or does a minimum effort, his payment is the same – one day of his obligation is fulfilled. If he were to make money on the side, he would only be making money for his master. Anything he produces belongs to the slave's master.

This is why a sinner cannot earn righteousness. He is a slave to sin, and anything accomplished belongs to sin. A sinner is in debt, and has no way to earn anything, thus making it impossible to merit his or her way out of debt to sin. Any good works still belongs to sin. Any evil works belongs to sin. He is in bondage and cannot earn freedom.

The opposite is also true. Those set free from sin are also in bondage to righteousness. They cannot break free or become indebted to another. Look at **Romans 6:18-20**

18 And having been set free from sin, you became slaves of righteousness.

19 I speak in human *terms* because of the weakness of your flesh. For just as you presented your members *as* slaves of

uncleanness, and of lawlessness *leading* to *more* lawlessness, so now present your members *as* slaves *of* righteousness for holiness.
[20] For when you were slaves of sin, you were free in regard to righteousness.

When you were in bondage to sin, you were free from righteousness. Righteousness had no claim over your life, and it could not claim you. You were enslaved to sin and were bound to sin with no power to break free. Then Christ, your kinsman Redeemer, came and bought you out of slavery, and took you from being bound to sin, and bound you to His righteousness.

This is a critical truth to understand. The Bible says that you were bought with a price and you are not your own. The Bible also says that you are now slaves of righteousness. Just as you could not be free from sin, regardless of what you did, you now cannot be free from righteousness.

Stop for a moment and ponder this truth. It is not your righteousness that makes you acceptable to God. It is God's righteousness given to you. You are the righteousness of God. You are not righteous for God. Just as you were once in the prison of slavery, you are now in the house of righteousness. You were bought with a price, and now you are a slave of righteousness.

A slave does not have the right to enter into debt, for he does not belong to himself. In the same way, you can never again be a slave of sin because you do not have the right to put yourself back under debt. It's impossible.

If a slave were to enter into a legal agreement and sign a contract putting himself in debt, his master would immediately nullify the contract. "He belongs to me and doesn't have the right to enter into a legal agreement. This agreement is null and void."

In the same way, if you commit a sin (the verb of sin), sin (the noun) cannot enslave you because it has no claim over God's possession.

This does not mean that sinning has no consequences. What it does mean is that sin has no rights over you. Nor do you have the right to surrender your soul to sin. You can submit to it, but it has no power over you. You can be bluffed into believing you are enslaved, but once you know the truth, it sets you free. The truth is that sin has no power over the Christian. It isn't human weakness that cause so many Christians to be ruled by sin; it is the lack of knowledge of the truth.

The moment you understand that you have been emancipated from sin, you can walk away from its power freely. And it cannot stop you.

This is something that most Christians do not understand, and something I did not understand for most of my Christian life. The sinful habits that I wrestled with most of my life fell away once I started walking in faith. The things I had no power to defeat suddenly had no power to defeat me. This is because I did not have to defeat my sins. Jesus has already accomplished this. But because I didn't understand this truth, I could not walk in faith.

"Walk in the Spirit and you will not fulfill the lusts of the flesh," **Galatians 5:16**

I didn't have to overcome the cravings of my flesh. I just needed to walk in the new life that was already mine, and the flesh had no power. The flesh has no power over the Christian – unless we set our minds in a fleshly way of thinking.

I'm going to use an illustration that I've used several times, but helps to give me a word picture of this truth.

One day, Jesus said to His disciples, "Get in the boat and go to the other side of the sea, and I will come to you." It was a command they could not fulfill. This is a picture of the law. The law commands us to do the impossible so that mankind can understand that this life is by the power of God and not ourselves. Mankind rowed against the wind for thousands of years until Christ came and He took His people to the other side, where the life of the Spirit is. This is given as a word-picture through this biblical illustration.

The disciples started off fine, but then a wind storm arose. For the next nine hours they rowed fruitlessly against the wind. The entire time, Jesus was on the mountain top watching. Just as they reached the point of exhaustion, Jesus came down, walked out on the troubled sea, and came to meet them.

They were in a dire situation, just fighting to keep from being swallowed by the sea. Jesus called out, "It is I, do not be afraid." Twelve men were in that boat of religion, but only one answered Jesus' call.

Peter said, "Bid me to come to you."

Jesus said, "Come." That call wasn't for Peter alone, but only Peter had ears to hear it because He was focused on Christ.

Peter stepped out of the boat and onto the raging sea as he looked to Jesus. Because he was focused on Christ, he discovered the sea had no power over him. The wind could not topple him, and the waves of despair became a firm foundation under his feet. For a few precious steps, Peter did what was humanly impossible. He walked in the Spirit and this life of the flesh had zero power against him. Then he took his eyes off Jesus and looked at the waves. Fear returned and the world claimed him in his life of the flesh.

Yet Jesus didn't abandon him. Christ reached into the sea, plucked Peter out, and they entered the boat, and they were immediately at the other side.

The people of the church sit in the boat and wait for Jesus to rescue us from sin and the world around us. Because of this, God's people never experience the power that God has built into our life of faith. Like the disciples of Jesus, we don't even need the boat. If the disciples had trusted Jesus and refused to look at the circumstances of life, they could have left the boat behind and enjoyed an amazing journey to the other side.

This is you and I. We pray for God's intervention and wait. Often we cry out in desperation, wondering why God takes so long to rescue our boat. Yet God's outside the boat asking us to step out in faith, calling us to look unto Jesus, the Author and Finisher of our faith.

Most people are afraid to escape the safety of religious regulations because it represents to them the protection of the boat. A few will occasionally step out of the boat and experience the miraculous. But our life in this world distracts us, and we fall from the power of grace. Jesus picks us up and says, "You were walking above it all. Why did you doubt? Why did you take your eyes off Me?" But He will not leave you in the waves for long.

Now here is the rarity of the Christian experience. Most people look at the failure of falling in the sea and say, "I'm not getting out of the boat again," when they should be looking at the miracle of what happened before they took their eyes off Christ.

You will fall. It's okay. No one learns how to walk in the Spirit without falling. Life distracts us. The winds of trouble threaten us. Our recognition that we are not supposed to be walking on water strikes us and we give in to doubt. Then we stop looking at Christ and fall. It's okay. Really, it is okay.

God lifts you up, instructs you not to doubt, and then calls you to step out again. It's hard not to get distracted. It's hard not to look at temptation, struggles, threats, and all the other things of this life. Many people will be calling you to get back in the boat. You might come back in the boat soaked and coughing, like Peter. Someone might have said to Peter, "What did you expect? It was stupid to get out of the boat."

What you need to do is look back at Christ and answer His call, "Come." As you learn to keep your focus on Him, your falls will become few and far between. Or you might go through a period of time where you have a hard time staying focused on Christ. Again I say, "It's okay." God wants you to keep growing and learning to walk by faith.

We walk by faith, not by sight. Faith is looking at Christ. Sight is looking at the world and our own abilities – or inabilities.

No child learns to walk without falling. They grow in the safety of holding on, then one day they let go of the couch and take a step. Then they fall. Their parents don't rush to them and yell, "You failed me!" That would be a bad parent. So why would we think God is doing this to us?

As children take longer steps of faith, they go farther and experience life from a new perspective. Yet they still fall from time to time. Sometimes they get hurt. Toddlers frequently get bruised and get knots on their head, but the more they learn to walk, the less often they fall.

God is pleased when you put your trust in His hands and step out in faith. Even when you fall, He is still pleased. Instead of scorning us when we fall, God gives us the promise of **Psalm 37:23-24**

> 23 The steps of a *good* man are ordered by the LORD, And He delights in his way.
> 24 Though he fall, he shall not be utterly cast down; For the LORD upholds *him with* His hand.

The good man (and woman) is the one who has been made the righteousness of God. That is you. God is directing your steps as you respond to His call to "Come." When you fall, God does not allow you to be destroyed. He plucks you out of the sea and upholds you with His hand. And notice the promise. God delights in your way – even though you fall!

This passage doesn't say, "if he falls," but "though he falls." You will fall, and God takes your hand to hold you up. And even when you stumble and fall, God delights leading you into the abundant life He has designed for you. God delights when you step out to answer His call. God delights in taking you from your weaknesses to teach you how to walk in the power of the Spirit. Let me reiterate again, God even delights in you when you fall. It's His pleasure to comfort you, build you back up, and encourage you to walk in His steps.

I'm challenging you to rethink the way you look at your weaknesses and struggles. What you consider to be a failure is the process of learning to leave the old behind and learn to walk in the new.

I'm also challenging you to rethink God's view of you. Since He has promised to never be angry at you, it's time to change your perception to understand how God looks at you. He views you the same way you would look at your own child, who is learning how to explore life outside the womb. You have been born again into a new life, but you have to explore the life of the Spirit in order to learn to walk in it.

Failure is not falling. Failure is staying in the safety of religion. Success comes to the one who falls and continues to get up. The Bible says that a wise person will fall, but always get up again. It does not say a wise man will never fall.

Rest in the truth that God's affections are upon you, and He delights in your way. He will not leave you in the flesh. Also rest in the truth that you are already an overcomer. Let's conclude with **1 John 5:4**

For whatever is born of God overcomes the world. And this is the victory that has overcome the world-- our faith.

The Bible does not merely say that you can be a conqueror, but that you are more than conquerors through Christ. The reason people don't experience this truth is because our victory is discovered through faith. You are learning how to trust in the work of Christ as you wean yourself off looking to the world, or looking to your own efforts.

Stop worrying about what you are doing, and start learning how to trust in the finished work of Christ, which has been given to you as a gift of God's love.

True faith trusts in God's love when we blow it. It is God that produces success in us, and that doesn't happen until we stop looking at us, and learn to look to Christ. True faith understands that my falls cannot defeat Christ's work. What God wants from you is trust in His love and promises. Without faith it is impossible to please God.[4] When you trust Him during your failures, you are pleasing Him. What's more, is as you learn to stay Christ-focused, He will transform your weaknesses into His strength.

---

[4] Hebrews 11:6

Reexamining the Law

A theologian on television echoes a commonly taught belief by saying, "Grace gives you the power to keep the law."

It's undeniable that the followers of the Old Testament could not keep the law. In John 7:19, Jesus said, "Did not Moses give you the law, yet none of you keeps the law?"

Think for a moment about the magnitude of that statement. The Jewish culture was built around the Old Testament law. Their government was focused on that law, all of their customs and cultures were built around the law, and the Jewish lifestyle was focused on the law. Yet even with everything focused on trying to keep the Old Testament law, not one of them was able to keep it.

When the New Covenant church was born, it soon spread outside of the Jewish world and Gentile churches were born. A Gentile is anyone who is not a Jew. The non-Jews were never under the law and did not even know the law. But the Jewish Christians had a difficult time accepting that the law was not the focus of the New Covenant. They began to go to Gentile churches and teach them that they could not be accepted by God unless they kept the law.

A dispute rose in the church, and all the early church leaders met to discuss the issue. Again, the Jewish Christian leaders acknowledged that the law was a burden that could not be fulfilled. The Apostle Peter stood up and said in **Acts 15:10**

> Now therefore, why do you test God by putting a yoke on the neck of the disciples which neither our fathers nor we were able to bear?

God had affirmed that the Gentiles had been accepted into the New Covenant of grace without the law (See Acts chapters 10 and 11). Since God made no distinction between those who came to Christ out of Judaism and those who came to Christ out of the Gentile world, it was a challenge to the work of God when people tried to put the burden of the law onto those whom Christ had already redeemed.

The same battle rages today. There are many movements that set aside grace by saying it's Jesus plus the law. But the Bible clearly refutes this idea.

Let's begin by defining grace. It's often defined as 'unmerited favor', but what does that mean? The Greek word 'grace' (charis) means the recompense or receiving the benefits of God's favor. Recompense is a reward or compensation for something – in our case, it's for our faith. We'll see that taught clearly.

Grace is not the power to do what Jesus has already done. Grace is the gift of God's love given to us through Christ, and through the Holy Spirit within us. Once we focus on what we must do, we are pushing aside what Christ has done. Look at **Galatians 2:21**

> I do not set aside the grace of God; for if righteousness *comes* through the law, then Christ died in vain.

Add to this the words of **Galatians 5:4-5**
> [4] You have become estranged from Christ, you who *attempt to* be justified by law; you have fallen from grace.
> [5] For we through the Spirit eagerly wait for the hope of righteousness by faith.

Rather than teaching us that grace gives us the power to keep the law, the Bible teaches that those who attempt to be justified by the law have fallen from grace. In the Greek, justify (justification) comes from the same root word as righteousness. The word justify/justification is the Greek word dikaioo, which means to be rendered righteous, or to be made righteous.

The word 'righteous' is the Greek word dikaiosune, which means to be in the state of righteousness. Justify is the action of God making us righteous, and righteousness is the state of being righteous, after God has performed His work.

It's important to understand this, for when God justifies us through faith, the Bible is declaring that God has performed the act of making us righteous. After this, we are declared as being the righteousness of God through Christ.

When we understand this truth, then it becomes clear that trying to become righteous is a declaration that we don't believe that God was indeed able to do what He has declared as a finished work through Christ. Why would I try to do what God has already said He has finished? Justification is a verb. It is the act of God transforming us into His righteousness. After this, we are called the noun of righteousness, indicating that God's action was a success. We are then called to first believe, and then to walk in God's finished work, which is His gift to us.

You are not trying to become righteous. You are trying to learn to walk by faith, where righteousness is revealed in all its glory in us. We are Christ-focused as we wait for the hope of righteousness by faith.[5] Faith in Christ. The word 'hope' in the Bible means: The confident expectation of good. Our hope is based on our confidence that God's work is sufficient, so we can trust in what He has provided.

Our common English vernacular says, "I hope so," when we are wishing that something might happen. This is not the meaning of hope in the Bible. Hope in scripture is the confident assurance of what we already know to be true. When you see hope in scripture, it means that you believe God's word, and you are confidently expecting the fulfillment of His promise – even when you don't yet see what He has declared as yours.

Take a moment and think about the one thing in your life that you wish you could change. It might be a bad temper, negative attitude, addiction, sinful habit, envy, bitter spirit, or anything you might be struggling with. The Bible isn't telling you to make yourself right with God (justification) by trying to stop sinning. You are instructed to believe in God's work of justification that has already been accomplished, and then to trust (faith) in Christ as you wait confidently for the promise of the Spirit's work in your life.

As the saying goes, the proof is in the pudding. If the traditionalist view worked, then why is sin still rampant in the

---

[5] Galatians 5:5

Reexamining the Law

church? If you've been in church for any length of time, you have likely seen the unveiling of the weakness of someone you looked up to as a spiritual leader. Sometimes the holiest appearing people show the worst behavior when they get under stress. How is it that people sit in church thirty and forty years, but are no more spiritually mature than they were decades ago?

Why did I try in vain to stop my sinful habits for most of my Christian life? I did everything I was told to do, but the best I could do was curb my behavior for a few weeks at a time, and hide my failures from those around me.

But something changed when I discovered the true meaning of grace. Instead of trying to make myself conform, I discovered that the secret of the Christian life was to trust in Christ's completed works. He had already done the work, and it was the Spirit's job to transform my mind, which then transformed my behavior. And it all centered around trusting in Christ as I waited expectantly for the Spirit to do in me what He had promised in His word.

This isn't possible outside of grace. Under the law, we are blinded to the gift of grace, and then left in the state of limited human abilities. Consider this passage in **2 Corinthians 3:14-18**

14 But their minds were blinded. For until this day the same veil remains unlifted in the reading of the Old Testament, because the *veil* is taken away in Christ.

15 But even to this day, when Moses is read, a veil lies on their heart.

16 Nevertheless when one turns to the Lord, the veil is taken away.

17 Now the Lord is the Spirit; and where the Spirit of the Lord *is*, there *is* liberty.

18 But we all, with unveiled face, beholding as in a mirror the glory of the Lord, are being transformed into the same image from glory to glory, just as by the Spirit of the Lord.

The statement, "When Moses is read," refers to the reading of the Old Testament law. When the Old Testament law is read, it becomes the veil that blinds us to the truth of grace. The moment you focus on the law, you have put a veil over your eyes, and that veil can never be lifted until you turn to Christ.

When Jesus fulfilled the law and then offered Himself up to the penalty of the law for us on the cross, an amazing thing happened. The veil of the temple was torn from the top to the bottom, indicating that God was the one removing the veil. The veil was the barrier between the people and God. God took away the veil of the temple, but religious mankind reinstituted the veil by covering our faces with the law. What God took away, religion tries to restore. Without faith, facing God is a fearful thing.

But we, with unveiled faces are beholding the glory of Christ, and as we behold His glory, the Spirit works to transform us into that same glory!

That's why I spent two decades trying in vain to live this Christian life and fruitlessly striving to overcome sin, but the moment I got a glimpse of the unveiled glory of Christ, my sins fell away like chains. It's also why we struggle in daily Christian life. Things distract us from Christ, and the power of the Spirit is only experienced as we behold the glory of Christ. His grace is His glory. Look at **Ephesians 1:6**

To the praise of the glory of His grace, by which He has made us accepted in the Beloved.

When you try to make yourself righteous, you are trying to glorify your flesh. The Bible says that God will not share His glory with another, yet God also promises to glorify us together with Himself. It's another great paradox of the Bible. Your glory is to become a partaker of God's glory. You don't produce your own, but instead, your glory is to be seated together with your Lord and enjoy His power working in you. It is not your power working for Him.

Human pride is greatly deceitful. When I believe I am succeeding for God, I believe my glory is of God. Believing that grace empowers me to keep the law is the same as believing that I can replace what Christ has done with what I do. It's almost like believing that God teaches me to craft my own righteousness.

People who believe in the law become hostile when the law is taken from them. Why? Why do religious people become angry when you tell them that everything is given to them by God, and nothing comes from themselves? It's because self-glorification has been taken away. Yet the pride of religion never believes man's works are rooted in pride.

In Jesus' day, the sinners loved the message of grace, but the religious people hated it. Prostitutes found hope. Drunkards found deliverance. Thieves discovered transformation. Yet the legalistic thinkers saw nothing but a threat and called grace evil. They redefined grace in a way that shifted the glory from Christ to their own works, which was a reflection on themselves.

At the heart of the fleshly nature is the desire to declare our worthiness to God, and an attempt to put Him in debt to us. God owes me a reward because of what I have done for Him.

This is why the law was given. The human mind reshapes the law into something we can keep so we feel reward-worthy. But Jesus came to show religion that the only reason they thought they were keeping the law is because they had lowered the bar. "You say you haven't committed adultery," Jesus said. "I tell you the truth, that if you've even looked at a woman and lusted in your heart, you have already committed adultery in your heart."

Jesus did this any time someone tried to make themselves righteous because of what they do. The rich young ruler thought he proved he loved his neighbor as himself because he gave more to the poor than other people did, thus believing he was more righteous by what he did. Jesus showed him that the command wasn't to do more than your neighbor. To fulfill this one burden of the law, he would have to sell everything and give to the poor. Even that would only satisfy one law.

The law was designed to show mankind that it is impossible to be like God. It was intended to be a burden to drive us to Christ, and once you are in Christ, the law relinquished its role over to the

Spirit – who is able to make us good by imparting God's righteousness into us as a gift of grace.

Equally important is to understand that the law came to an end in Christ. If you are in Christ, you have fulfilled the whole law. Let's examine passages that explain this, and rethink how we view the law. Let's begin with **Romans 8:3-4**

> [3] For what the law could not do in that it was weak through the flesh, God *did* by sending His own Son in the likeness of sinful flesh, on account of sin: He condemned sin in the flesh,
> [4] that the righteous requirement of the law might be fulfilled in us who do not walk according to the flesh but according to the Spirit.

What was the weakest link of the law? It was you and me. In order to fulfill the law, we would have to be on the same level of righteousness as the law, but the weakness of the law is the flesh – our human nature that rules us outside of Christ.

But Christ not only fulfilled the law, but also fulfilled the law in you because you are in Him. The righteous requirement of the law is fulfilled in you in the Spirit, not in you through human effort (or the flesh). You fulfilled the law by faith, because you are entering into Christ work. Because you are in Christ, you have the benefit of what He accomplished.

If the Bible says you have fulfilled the law, what are you trying to accomplish by attempting to keep rules and regulations? Is that not a denial of what Christ has done?

At this point, critics of grace claim that if we don't work to fulfill the law, we'll fall back into sin. Yet we just read that if we are Christ focused, the Spirit works in us to transform us into His likeness. We don't have that promise if we focus on the law. In fact, if you go on to read the entire chapter of Romans 8, it compares keeping the law as setting our minds in the flesh. This is the Bible's declaration of the fulfillment Jesus promised in **Matthew 5:17-18**

> [17] "Do not think that I came to destroy the Law or the Prophets. I did not come to destroy but to fulfill.

Reexamining the Law

¹⁸ "For assuredly, I say to you, till heaven and earth pass away, one jot or one tittle will by no means pass from the law till all is fulfilled.

No one could escape the burden of the law until it was fulfilled, which Jesus promised to do in Matthew 5:17. Jesus didn't destroy the law, He fulfilled it. And now that He fulfilled it, we are called into faith where we are under His works, which means we have fulfilled the law.

Our options are simple. We can be under our own works, and try to fulfill the law, which not one person in history could do, other than Christ. The reason Christ could fulfill it was because He was already righteous and His fulfillment was a reflection of His divine nature. But those under their own works are also under the penalty of the law. The Bible says that if we keep the whole law, but fail in one point, we are guilty of the entire law. Under the law, our shortcomings are sin, and the wages of sin is death.

Our second option is to be under Jesus' work, where the law has been fulfilled, and because we are in the Spirit of grace, the righteous requirements of the law is fulfilled in us because we are in Him.

Let's examine a few passages that teach us of the end result of Jesus' promise to fulfill the law. Look now at **Romans 10:3-4**

³ For they being ignorant of God's righteousness, and seeking to establish their own righteousness, have not submitted to the righteousness of God.
⁴ For Christ *is* the end of the law for righteousness to everyone who believes.

Those focused on the law are ignorant (or don't understand) God's righteousness. Since they don't understand that righteousness is God's gift to us, they set aside the grace of God and seek to establish their own righteousness. Which, by the way, is impossible. The Bible says that human righteous acts are filthy rags in God's sight. The reason is that human effort is empowered by sinful flesh, and cannot produce the righteousness of God.

But those who believe in the gospel have an amazing promise. Jesus Christ is the end of the law for righteousness to everyone who believes. To believe is to walk in faith, receiving what God has provided as gifts of love, which is grace. Righteousness is part of God's gift of grace to you. Those who don't believe focus on keeping the law. Those who do believe, focus on Christ and are justified, holy, sanctified, and righteous.

If that weren't enough, we have the promise of **Romans 5:13**
For until the law sin was in the world, but sin is not imputed when there is no law.

Before the law, sin was in the world. There was consequences to sin, but God did not impute sin to mankind, which means He didn't judge men's souls against their sin. There was no law to condemn, so God did not condemn. Now that Jesus has brought an end to the law, there again is no law to condemn.

I can't leave this topic without looking at the three-fold blessing given to those who are in faith. After explaining that Abraham was credited with righteousness because He believed God, the Apostle Paul goes on to explain the Old Testament foretelling of our blessed life of faith. Pay close attention to what the Bible tells us we are blessed with below. **Romans 4:6-8**
⁶ just as David also describes the blessedness of the man to whom God imputes righteousness apart from works:
⁷ "Blessed *are those* whose lawless deeds are forgiven, And whose sins are covered;
⁸ Blessed *is the* man to whom the LORD shall not impute sin."

The first blessing is that those who are in Christ are imputed with righteousness, apart from their works or deeds. That's what we have been studying. You are the righteousness of God in Christ, for God has imputed, or credited to your account, His own righteousness because you believed His word, that Christ has completed your salvation. Not part, but all of your salvation.

The second blessing is that your sins were forgiven. Your unrighteous acts were forgiven and covered by the blood of Christ. Your old sins were forgiven, and because the law has been removed, no new sin can be laid against you.

And this is the third blessing. Blessed are you because the Lord will not impute sin to you. Where there is no law, sin cannot be imputed. Sin is still in the world, and those who live in sin will still have to deal with its consequences, but you can never again be brought under condemnation to sin. This is why we have the promise of **Romans 8:1-2**

> [1] *There is* therefore now no condemnation to those who are in Christ Jesus, who do not walk according to the flesh, but according to the Spirit.
> [2] For the law of the Spirit of life in Christ Jesus has made me free from the law of sin and death.

There is a law you are under. The Bible calls it the law of faith. Here it is called the law of the Spirit of life in Christ Jesus. Because you are under this law, you cannot be under the old law of sin and death. That only exists outside Christ. Since there is no law of sin and death, you cannot be brought back under condemnation.

Some will argue that this only applies to those who are behaving, but you are in the Spirit, regardless of your behavior. Certainly, you can invest your life in this world where everything is destined to perish, but that still doesn't nullify the promise. Look at **Romans 8:9-11**

> [9] But you are not in the flesh but in the Spirit, if indeed the Spirit of God dwells in you. Now if anyone does not have the Spirit of Christ, he is not His.
> [10] And if Christ *is* in you, the body *is* dead because of sin, but the Spirit *is* life because of righteousness.
> [11] But if the Spirit of Him who raised Jesus from the dead dwells in you, He who raised Christ from the dead will also give life to your mortal bodies through His Spirit who dwells in you.

You are not in the flesh, but in the Spirit if you have received Christ. In other books, I discuss this more in-depth, but we can put our minds in the flesh and never experience the abundant life or victory over sin, but that does not mean we haven't been given righteousness and made overcomers by the success of Christ.

Your body is still dead to sin, but you have a new spirit born of God and that has the life of Christ. If you live in the flesh, you will experience the same life you had in the flesh. But if you are looking to Christ and walking by faith, you will experience the life of the Spirit.

Though your body is still part of this corrupted world, your spirit has the life of God's Spirit because of righteousness. As we have been studying, it's because of God's righteousness put within you, not because your behavior has earned righteousness. Just as sin brings death, God's righteousness brings life. You are alive in Christ because of what God has invested into you.

To summarize it all, you were given the promise that the same life that raised Jesus from the dead lives in you, and He gives life to your mortal bodies.[6] Some apply this to mere physical healing, but don't short-change this promise.

Remember the promise that you are transformed into Jesus' glory as you behold Him? This applies to that promise. The Spirit of God within you has the power to raise you from the dead works of the flesh and into the abundant life of the Spirit. You don't have this promise in the law. You don't have this promise by trying your best for God. Sin and the things that hinder you have no power against the Spirit. You will be raised into new life, but only when your life is walking by faith, looking to Jesus, and resting in the hope of His promises.

Very few Christians experience this because it is outside human understanding. How can just looking unto Jesus make me stop sinning? It doesn't. It submits your mind to faith, where the Spirit transforms your mind into the same glory that already resides

---

[6] Romans 8:11

in your new spirit. This promise is to those who believe. The law is not of faith.[7] Meditate on **Galatians 3:10-12**

[10] For <u>as many as are of the works of the law are under the curse</u>; for it is written, "Cursed *is* everyone who does not continue in all things which are written in the book of the law, to do them."

[11] But that <u>no one is justified by the law</u> in the sight of God *is* evident, for "the just shall live by faith."

[12] Yet <u>the law is not of faith</u>, but "the man who does them shall live by them."

The law is not of faith. Those who try to live by the works of the law are submitting themselves under the curse of the law. No one is pleasing to God because of the works of the law. The Bible says that if we live by works, it is no longer grace.[8] Someone once asked this question, "Wouldn't it be safer to keep the law in case that's what God wants?"

No. That's like saying, "Shouldn't we trust in ourselves, in case Christ didn't do enough?" We are told not to set aside the grace of God for works. We are also told the following in **Hebrews 10:38**

Now the just shall live by faith; But if *anyone* draws back, My soul has no pleasure in him."

God has no pleasure in the works of those who draw back from faith, and submit to the law, which is NOT of faith. It's hard to walk by faith when the religious world around us has a conflicting message. When we draw back from faith, we cannot please God, and we have seen that faith is not of works. Let's conclude this chapter with **Hebrews 11:6**

But without faith *it is* impossible to please *Him*, for he who comes to God must believe that He is, and *that* He is a rewarder of those who diligently seek Him.

---

[7] Galatians 3:12
[8] Romans 11:6

Where is the law? Where is works? Does God say He is not pleased if we don't do enough works? Or if we don't fulfill the law? No. Without faith it is impossible to please God, and if we draw back from trusting in the completed work of Christ, God has no pleasure in our religion or efforts.

You are not rewarded because of what you do. You are rewarded because you believe, and you have enough faith to seek the Lord, knowing that all His promises are your hope. Even good works / deeds are the work of the Spirit through us. Your only task is to look at Christ, and seek Him. The person who does this CANNOT miss the pleasure of God and will not come short in any gift or work. This is the Christian life. The burden lies on the Lord, and His promises rest on you.

The Ark – a Picture of Christ

The Bible says that the law is good – if it is used correctly. The things in the Old Testament are either pictures of Christ, or they are foreshadowing what He was to fulfill. After the crucifixion, two of His followers were walking from Jerusalem to Emaus, sad because the one they thought would redeem them had been killed.

Jesus joined them on the long walk, but they didn't recognize Him. Jesus said, "Oh you who are slow of heart to believe what was written by the prophets." He explained how the Old Testament scriptures showed why it was necessary for Christ to die. The Bible then says Jesus took them from the books of Moses (the first five books of the Old Testament), and throughout all the books of the prophets, explaining how the scriptures were speaking about things concerning Himself. Before the cross, everything written ultimately directs us to the coming work of Christ. In other words, the Old Testament points ahead to the cross.

Now that we are on the backside of the cross, we can look through the lens of the cross and see Jesus on each page of the Old Testament.

This is what it means to use the law correctly. All the things in the Old Covenant (or Old Testament Law), were shadows, or representations, of the true work that would be revealed in Christ. Let's see this in the Bible. Look first at **Hebrews 8:4-5**

> [4] For if He [Christ] were on earth, He would not be a priest, since there are priests who offer the gifts according to the law;
>
> [5] who serve the copy and shadow of the heavenly things...
>
> ...
>
> [13] In that He says, "A new *covenant*," He has made the first obsolete. Now what is becoming obsolete and growing old is ready to vanish away.

Hebrews 10:1
For the law, having a shadow of the good things to come,

and not the very image of the things, can never with these same sacrifices, which they offer continually year by year, make those who approach perfect.

I encourage you to read these chapters completely. I jumped around to point out a common theme. The law was a shadow, and not the real thing. There are many other passages that explain this. Galatians tells us that the law was our tutor that brought us to Christ, but after faith has come, there is no more a need for the tutor.

Studying the Old Testament is a great way to get a picture of Christ, but we have to understand that it all points to Christ and His completed work. Many amazing pictures of Christ can be found in the Old Testament. These help us to understand the work of Jesus. A great example of this is the Ark of the Covenant.

The Ark of the Covenant was built according to specific guidelines that God gave Moses. Moses was the Old Testament prophet that God used to lead the people out of slavery in Egypt. This also is a picture of Christ. Pharaoh is a picture of Satan's oppression, who heaps burdens on those under slavery to sin. Moses entered into Pharaoh's courts to declare that God was calling His people out of slavery in Egypt. He didn't fight Pharaoh; He proclaimed God's deliverance.

God broke Pharaoh's strength, led the people out of Egypt, through the Red Sea, and into the Promised Land. The Bible says that passing through the sea was a picture of baptism.

This was a foreshadow of Christ, who entered into Satan's domain, proclaimed the captives were now free, and led His people out of sin's bondage and to the promise of God. Baptism is a picture of the death, burial, and resurrection of Christ. We are baptized as a testimony that we have died to the old life, were buried with Christ, and are raised into new life. Our death to the old is shown in the Ark of the Covenant, as we shall soon see.

When Moses built the tabernacle of worship and the Ark of the Covenant, God instructed him to build it according to the pattern in heaven. On the mountain, God revealed the pattern,

The Ark – a Picture of Christ

which we now can clearly see was a picture of Christ's completed work of the New Covenant. It's also an amazing testimony that gives us great confidence in God's presence.

The Ark was built out of wood. Wood is perishable and has no eternal value. To protect the wood, God instructed the people to use beaten gold to be used to overlay the wood, inside and out. Inside the Ark, Moses was to place the tablets of stone, which is the law. They also put the testimonies of God in the Ark – a jar of manna and the rod that budded when the people demanded proof that Aaron was God's selected priest.

The lid of the Ark was to be made of solid gold. On top of the lid was the mercy seat, also made of gold, and two angels of gold with their wings touching over the mercy seat. Their faces were to be looking at the mercy seat.

When a sin offering was made, the High Priest was to take a lamb without blemish, slay it, and sprinkle the Ark with the blood of the lamb. On the Day of Atonement, God's people brought a spotless lamb to the priest. The priest did not examine the sinner; he examined the lamb. Once the lamb was determined as acceptable, the person was accepted, and they placed their hands on the lamb as a symbolic transfer of their sins to the lamb. Then the lamb was sacrificed for their sins. The lamb received the wages of sin, which is death, and the sinner walked away justified. The lamb was accounted as sin for the person, and the person was accounted as innocent because of the lamb. The blood of the lamb was applied to the mercy seat, testifying that man's sins were covered because the penalty was paid by the lamb.

This is a picture of salvation. The Bible tells us that Jesus is the Lamb of God. Jesus was examined by the priests at His trial and put to death even though the Roman governor examined Christ and said, "I find no fault in this man."

What the people didn't understand is that the Lamb of God was examined and found worthy, and our sins were transferred to Him. God does not examine us; He examines Christ. Once Jesus was declared as faultless, we were accepted by God because of the Lamb.

According to the Bible, Jesus sprinkled His blood on the altar in Heaven, once and for all. The shadow of Christ (the Ark) had to be sprinkled every year as a representation of the people's sins being covered. It wasn't an eternal sacrifice, so it had to be done yearly. However, Jesus' sacrifice is eternal, so it was done once and for all. He was the Lamb of God, who took away the sins of the whole world.

The wooden box is a picture of man's corruption, and the law that condemns us. Our testimony is a remembrance of where we came from, and what God has done. The gold covering the wood is a picture of pure righteousness covering our corruptible lives. The mercy seat, which was solid gold, is the picture of Christ. He is pure gold / pure righteousness, but we are merely covered by His righteousness.

Our human lives are still limited, but our sins cannot be seen because the gold has covered us. On heaven's side, there is no wood, only pure gold, pointing to our complete redemption through Christ. Even though we may be perishable like wood, the only thing God sees is the pure righteousness of Christ that has covered us.

Here is another amazing truth. Keep in mind, inside the Ark was the stone tablets of the law, a jar of manna, and the rod of Aaron that budded. It was the law that condemned man, the evidence of man's rebellion against the priest upholding the law, and the evidence of man's starving souls in the wilderness.

According to Colossians chapter 2, Jesus crucified us together with Himself. He also took our sins upon Himself. Not only that, but the Bible says that the law, which was the handwriting of ordinances that was against us, Jesus also nailed to His cross. The complete picture is that everything that corrupted us, accused us, and condemned us was put into the grave with Christ, and then we were raised together with Him in newness of life. The law, sin, and our old nature was put into the grave and declared as dead with Christ. We are now out of the grave and in the life of the Spirit.

This is clearly seen in the Ark of the Covenant. The Ark comes from the Hebrew word, 'arown', literally meaning 'coffin'. It's the same word used in **Genesis 50:26**

So Joseph died, *being* one hundred and ten years old; and they embalmed him, and he was put in a coffin in Egypt.

That word 'coffin' is the same word used for the 'Ark' of the Covenant. The Ark of the Covenant is a foreshadow of the grave of Christ, where the law and the evidence of our rebellion was covered by the mercy seat of Christ, and put into the grave/coffin where it is now dead and buried. Nothing inside the Ark can be seen unless we move the mercy seat out of the way.

Our sins were washed by the sacrifice of Christ, and that work was only done once because it is eternal. There is no such thing as re-applying the blood. This is why the Bible tells us that we are under Christ's eternal redemption. Redemption means that our debt was paid, and eternal redemption means it is forever paid and we cannot again be put under sin's debt.

The law is covered by the mercy seat, and it cannot be held against us. Jesus covered the law with His work. Beaten gold is a picture of His suffering, where He was beaten by the soldiers and nailed to the cross, where His blood was shed – and then offered for our sins, once and for all.

There is ONLY one way to see the law after the cross. We have to push grace aside in order to move the mercy seat and gaze upon the law. That means that we are pushing aside the blessing in order to gain access to the curse. The law is called our curse. The Old Testament gives a perfect picture of this in 1 Samuel 6.

The people had turned from the Lord, and during a war with their enemies, the Ark was taken by the Philistines. When the Philistines put the Ark under the idol of their God, the Lord plagued them until they relented and sent it back to Israel.

The people who received the Ark did something that brought judgment down. They lifted the mercy seat off the Ark and pushed it aside, and they looked at the stone tablets of the law. They received the curse of the law, and many people died.

This is an amazing picture of the law verses grace. The reason why sin can't be defeated in most Christian's lives is because we are taught to look at the law. That means we have to push aside the mercy seat, a picture of grace, and turn back to the law that Jesus covered. And the law does not bring a blessing, but a curse. This is explained in **Galatians 3:10**

For as many as are of the works of the law are under the curse; for it is written, "Cursed *is* everyone who does not continue in all things which are written in the book of the law, to do them."

To avoid the curse of the law, you must do and continue in ALL things written in the law. The Old Testament saints couldn't do it, even though they had a society built around the law. You certainly can't do it. Even if you could, one sinful thought would drop you back into the curse.

Why does anyone want to live under a system that demands perfection, and push aside Jesus, who has given us His perfection? Take to heart the words of **Galatians 2:21**

I do not set aside the grace of God; for if righteousness *comes* through the law, then Christ died in vain.

If righteousness could have come through the law, then there was no need for Christ to have died. Those who look to the law are setting aside the grace of God in order to reach the law. They are moving the mercy seat of redemption away, and demanding to be judged according to their own works.

This is the word-picture we are given in 1 Samuel 6. Those who moved aside the grace of God received the curse. This is also why so few Christians discover the abundant life of rest in Christ.

The picture of the Ark is intended to be a great encouragement to you. Your sin is with the law, covered by the mercy seat of Christ. Unless you push Christ aside, there is nothing that can condemn you again. The New Testament took everything that can condemn you out of the way. Look at **Colossians 2:13-15**

¹³ And you, being dead in your trespasses and the uncircumcision of your flesh, He has made alive together with Him, having forgiven you all trespasses,

¹⁴ having wiped out the handwriting of requirements that was against us, which was contrary to us. And He has taken it out of the way, having nailed it to the cross.

¹⁵ Having disarmed principalities and powers, He made a public spectacle of them, triumphing over them in it.

Circumcision is the cutting away of your old sinful nature. Your old nature was nailed to the cross and buried under the mercy seat. Your sins were removed by Jesus nailing it to the cross so you could be forgiven by the sprinkling of His blood. It also was buried under the mercy seat. Finally, the handwriting of requirements against you, which is the law, was nailed to the cross, and buried under the mercy seat of Christ.

This is why all principalities were disarmed. Satan's only power over you came through the condemnation of the law. The law was his weapon against you, but now he is disarmed and powerless. He can only be the voice of deception that tries to persuade you to turn from Christ and reach for the curse of the law.

But God has better things in store for you. When you are under the voice of condemnation, look to the mercy seat of Christ and rest in the fact that sin is no longer visible. When you hear words of condemnation, point to the blood on the mercy seat. Look to Christ. Then rest in the promise of Romans 8:1, "There is now no condemnation to those who are in Christ Jesus."

The Ark of the Covenant is not a picture of the law, but of the grace of Jesus Christ. You are seated with Him and there is nothing to condemn you; however, there is much that has been promised to you for your hope – or confident expectation of God's good for you!

You are worthy because you are seated with Christ on the mercy seat, and everything that disqualified you is in the coffin. You are covered by the pure gold of Christ's righteousness. It's time to stop peeking under the mercy seat and start resting in the assurance of His mercy.

Rethinking Self-Worth

The problem with self-help books is that they try to persuade us to believe something about us that we doubt is true. At the heart of self-help ideology is the same problem that we find in legalism and other forms of religion. It is focused on self.

Since self-help is self-focused, it depends on the ability of self-deception. People who see their own flaws go to motivational tapes and self-help books in an attempt to convince themselves to believe the mirage of so-called confidence boosters. They are trying to learn how to distance themselves from what they already believe is true – namely, that they are lacking in value.

When I was younger, a very attractive woman criticized her appearance. She said, "Look at my nose. It makes me look ugly." She saw a flaw that no one else could see. This is even more true when it comes to our character flaws. You and I can see weaknesses in ourselves that others cannot see.

I'll let you in on a little secret. If you try to find self-worth or a positive self-identity by looking at yourself, you will fall short. It's no coincidence that most mental health issues have a self-identity crisis at the heart. The people with the lowest self-confidence are the ones who become the most angry when they feel insulted or slighted. They may project a façade of confidence, but they are standing on very fragile egos. Anyone who bases their worth on their ego – or self-identity, is on a fragile foundation.

Almost as fragile is the person whose self-identity is based on the acceptance of another person of flesh. Every person has been created with an inner need of belonging. Friendship, love, and other relationships build our sense of belonging. But what if someone is not loved by the person they want to be connected to? Whether it's a close friend, or a romantic relationship, no one can be responsible for your healthy self-image. Love doesn't demand. Selfishness demands, but it often masquerades as love. This is why the Bible says, "Cursed is the man who puts his trust in man." You are setting yourself up for failure when you put your trust in people, who are just as flawed and have the same needs as you do.

Love is the response of what is gifted. It cannot be forced, manipulated, or exist in the vacuum of a fantasy. Love thrives when one person gives of themselves, and the other receives that gift, and gives of themselves. Love doesn't demand; it gives. Two givers have a healthy relationship. Two people trying to take love sucks the life out of a relationship. Love cannot survive in a demanding heart.

Love is one of the greatest builders of self-worth we can discover. The reason someone feels insecure is because they don't feel accepted, and they project the feeling of rejection upon their own identity. This is why there are dozens of self-motivation books, but so little success. I can tell myself I am valuable all I want, but if there is nothing other than myself to affirm that value, it is a house of glass. One discouragement and our ego shatters. If our identity is dependent on the affirmation of another person, then one failure on their part creates resentment in us because our sense of worth is not being fulfilled.

Satan always attacks our self-worth. Sometimes this attack comes through people, but the majority of the time, your worth is attacked through a misguided focus on self.

When we are trying to find meaning, it's an inner need that causes us to realize there is more to life. So what happens if we try to fulfill our inner need by looking to our self? We can't fulfill a need by looking to the needy. My needy heart will not have the answers or the supply.

It is also dangerous to look to another person, for they are trying to fulfill their own lack. It's unfair for someone to put the burden of their happiness upon us, and it's unfair for us to put that burden on someone else. They have the same needs, though it may be expressed in different ways.

This is why condemnation is so destructive. Self-condemnation is at the heart of all identity struggles. If I feel condemned, it damages how I view myself, and it makes a healthy emotional and spiritual life impossible.

This is why the greatest spiritual attacks will come through feelings of condemnation. If the enemy makes us feel condemned, we will not experience the love of God, and everything in the Christian life is birthed through God's love for us. The enemy condemns; the Spirit of God builds up.

Everything in the New Covenant centers around our acceptance by God. The New Covenant began at the cross. Sometimes Jesus used the law to condemn religion, but this was only the revelation that acceptance does not come through human effort. It is God's love, given freely to us.

What people don't realize is that the purpose of sin is to reveal God's love to us. This may sound odd, but it is true. If you could make yourself righteous for God, then His love would be a response to what you could give Him. But once you realize that there is nothing you can give God, yet the love of God is poured into you, then it becomes clear that God loves you because He is love.

Your abilities are not what makes you valuable. It is God's love that makes you valuable.

When my oldest daughter was a baby, she had a plush Tweety-bird toy she loved. She liked to pick little fuzz balls off it, so by the time she was a toddler, Tweety had a bad case of the mange. He had big plastic eyes. Over the years, she dropped Tweety so many times that his eyes broke in several pieces. I glued them back on. I jokingly called him Franken-Tweety because he looked so damaged.

My daughter loved and cherished that tattered old Tweety toy. She carried him everywhere. One day I was paying for a meal at a restaurant, and my daughter walked up to the counter. She was too small to be seen, but up popped Franken-Tweety. The cashier gasped. "What happened to Tweety?" she said with a shock.

My daughter beamed with pride. "That's MY Tweety," she boasted. She's in her Twenties and still has that Tweety.

What gave Tweety his value? The world would have tossed him in the trash, but my daughter loved that toy, and it became the most treasured possession she had. There wasn't a toy in the world she would have traded him for. The value of Tweety was immeasurable, but his value came from the love of my daughter and not from the material that he was built out of.

You are God's treasure, and there isn't anything in the world that God would trade you away for. In fact, God traded His life for you. **Romans 5:8-10**

> [8] But God demonstrates His own love toward us, in that while we were still sinners, Christ died for us.
>
> [9] Much more then, having now been justified by His blood, we shall be saved from wrath through Him.
>
> [10] For if when we were enemies we were reconciled to God through the death of His Son, much more, having been reconciled, we shall be saved by His life.

Your value comes from God's love. Let me give another illustration. There was a man who received a distress call from a boat caught in a storm at sea. A helicopter pilot attempted to do a rescue, but the wind was so bad, he decided it was too risky to endanger his life and the life of his men. He wasn't willing to lose the lives of his crew of six to save one or two people on the capsized boat, but then he received some information that changed his mind. His son was on the distressed boat.

Love changed everything. It wasn't just a life at sea, it was someone he loved and would risk everything to save.

Why do you think sinners were so drawn to Jesus? Do you realize that Jesus never called a single prostitute, drunkard, or thief a sinner? One of my favorite stories is the woman at the well. She was an outcast among outcasts.

The woman was a Samaritan, which was a half-breed Jew. Maintaining a pure bloodline was important to the Jews. The Samaritans were the descendants of Jews who married outside of their nation during the era when Israel was scattered. When the nation came back to the land, these were they who had married from the nations around them, so they were exiled from the people. Jews hated Samaritans. When they wanted to disgrace another Jew, they called them a Samaritan as an insult.

If a Samaritan was wounded on the street, a Jewish man would walk on the opposite side of the street to avoid him. The Samaritan woman was born into this disgraced title. But then she became disgraced even among the other Samaritans. Divorce was unheard of in that era. Yet she had been divorced five times. Living with a man who wasn't your husband was unthinkable, yet this woman was living with a man she was not married to.

In that era, there was no plumbing, so the women would gather by the well to socialize and draw the day's water. By the time the sun grew hot, no one would be at the well. The Samaritan woman came to the well at the heat of the day to avoid the gossiping women. She was worthless in a society of misfits.

Jesus sent his disciples to run an errand, and He went to the well during the heat of the day. It was God meeting the woman where she was. Jesus did not condemn her. He showed her love and acceptance. He changed her life. She was so impacted by the man who would show value in her that she brought the people of the village to find the man who told her everything she did, yet without condemnation.

This woman did not feel self-worth. She was condemned by all, and especially by herself. Five failed marriages showed that she was trying to find worth through men, and as she drained the life out of the relationship, each marriage died. She was trying to find someone that would make her feel valued, but no man could fill the hole in her soul.

Then she found that she was valued. Her life blossomed when she found her worth in Christ. His love revealed that she was treasured by God. Jesus journeyed into the hated city, to the well in the uncomfortable heat, to find a despised woman, so he could restore her to life with the love of God. She became valuable the moment she recognized God's love for her.

This is why condemnation is so destructive. The law condemns, but God does not. God stepped into the law, took its condemnation, and then gives us the life-restoring gift of love. You are valuable because you are loved by God. While sin had made you an enemy of God, He loved you so much that He took your sin upon Himself, and declared you to be His valued child.

Then the Bible says, "If God did this while we were enemies, how much more are we saved through His life?" If God loved you this much when you were not His, how much more assurance you should have now that you are His treasure!

Don't believe the lie of condemnation! You are valuable because the greatest measure of value has been placed in you. You are God's Tweety.

I cherished my daughter's Tweety because she loved it so much. I looked after it because of her. How much more true is that about God? There is a reason why the Bible tells us that anyone who is in God's love will love one another. When I see how much God loves you, I will also value you because of Him. We are in the same love of God.

Also, don't believe the lie that you must love God enough. The law said, "You must love God with all your heart, mind, soul, and strength." As we have seen, the law was designed to show mankind that life isn't about what He can do, but what God has done. The demand of love was only to reveal to us that our love is limited and conditional. We are incapable of loving God with all of anything. The law said, "Are you good enough?" Grace says, "It was never about you to begin with." Look at **1 John 4:10**

In this is love, not that we loved God, but that He loved us and sent His Son *to be* the propitiation for our sins.

It's not about how well you can love God. It's about His love for you. A few verses later explains that we love Him because God first loved us. When God fills your heart with His agape love, you enter into His love and your love is a response to the abundance of His love for you. Here is your role in loving God. Look at **Jude 1:20-21**

[20] But you, beloved, building yourselves up on your most holy faith, praying in the Holy Spirit,

Rethinking Self-Worth

²¹ keep yourselves in the love of God, looking for the mercy of our Lord Jesus Christ unto eternal life.

You don't have to build your faith; you build yourself upon your most holy faith, which is God's gift to you. It is most holy because it originates from the Most Holy God. Through the gift of faith, you learn to look to the Lord, and your role is to keep yourself in the love of God. Abide in God's love for you.

Stop worrying about trying to love God. Rest in God's love for you. The work of love in you will take care of your love for God. The more you see how much you are loved, the more your heart will respond to His love.

Condemnation is self-focused. Diminished self-worth is the natural reaction to looking at yourself instead of at God. Religious rules distract us from love. No one has to make themselves love. No one finds self-worth by looking at themselves. If I feel worthless, how can I find worth by looking at myself?

When you believe in God's love for you, you will feel valued because of God's value in you. You will be confident because you will be Christ-confident. The Christian life thrives when that person trusts in God's declaration of love over them. Consider **1 John 4:16**

And we have known and believed the love that God has for us. God is love, and he who abides in love abides in God, and God in him.

How do you feel close to God? Abide in His love. Let God love you. Receive His love poured out upon you. All you need to worry about is abiding in God's love for you. Let God worry about the rest.

You were so loved by God, that when you were living for yourself and sin was ruling you, God died for you. Sin gave the law the right to condemn you, but since you were God's beloved, He stepped into your place and took that condemnation upon Himself. If that doesn't convince you that God loves you, what else is there?

Why should you believe the voice of condemnation when the words of God have called you His treasure and beloved?

His love proves your worth and value. Lack of self-worth and the lack of self-confidence is the evidence that you have lost sight of God's love for you. When you look at yourself, you will find areas of shame and failure. When you look to the Lord, you find what you lack, and He perfects you. Every failure becomes an opportunity to experience God's success.

When Jesus was arrested and led away to be crucified, all the disciples abandoned him except John. Before the soldiers came, the disciples were declaring their love for God, and Peter stood up and declared that his love was greater than them all. Then he found out his love was insufficient, and the one who declared the greatest love became the one who denied Jesus three times.

Five times in John's gospel, John calls himself, "The disciple Jesus loved." He was focused on Jesus' love for him, and that love gave him the strength to endure. John was the only disciple standing, and Jesus called on him to care for His mother while He was on the cross.

Do you want to be close to God? You will not be strengthened for ministry until you first are established in His love for you. When you understand that YOU are the disciple Jesus loves, you'll also realize that you are valued by God, and you will understand your worth without needing people or circumstances to affirm you.

God's worth will empower you when people fail. When you see limitations in yourself, the love of God becomes the strength that overcomes what you lack. In truth, you lack nothing – unless you are looking to yourself instead of to Christ.

Rethinking Worship

Often times the church turns praise and worship into a work of human effort, when true worship is a response of a heart overwhelmed with the greatness of God.

Well-meaning worship leaders often use guilt as a tool to persuade people to worship, but is this truly worship? The topic of worship is the final chapter of this book for a reason. My hope is that at this point, because you now see how much love and grace God is giving you, you are saying, "How can I keep from singing?"

Let's take a moment to revisit the concept of parenting. What does a parent do for their children? They work hard to provide. Food is on the table, clothes are provided, a home is provided, toys are given, and outings or vacations are planned. All of these are acts of love we focus toward our children.

It's not uncommon for children to take what they have for granted, and not even recognize how much sacrifice has been made on their behalf. It's often a thankless job, but let me ask a question. Which is thanksgiving, a mother or father demanding their child to tell them, "Thank you," or a child saying thanks because they recognize what a parent has given, and want to express appreciation?

I can demand my children praise my sacrifice. I can even threaten to take something from them if they don't thank me. To keep their benefit, they might reluctantly say, "Thanks," but would that make me feel appreciated? To me, it would be hollow words with little value.

Why do we tell people that they 'should' be praising God? Why do we try to force worship and make people feel that God will be displeased with them if they don't sing insincere words?

We have often created the false image of an egotistical, narcissistic god who demands to be worshipped or else. Do you really think God is looking down from a throne and saying, "You WILL worship Me or else?"

It's time to rethink worship. What God desires is for you to see how much He loves you. When you see the greatness of His sacrifice, the intricate planning of your life He has woven into creation, and the abounding grace He pours out on you, that's when you will be driven to praise. Look at **Psalm 139:16-18**

> [16] Your eyes saw my substance, being yet unformed. And in Your book they all were written, The days fashioned for me, When *as yet there were* none of them.
> [17] How precious also are Your thoughts to me, O God! How great is the sum of them!
> [18] *If* I should count them, they would be more in number than the sand

How much sand is in the ocean? That's a picture of how much thought God has put into your life in order to lead you into the abundance of His grace.

This is true, even for those who have gotten what we would call a raw deal. God has promised to restore the years that the world has consumed. To the one who will trust Him to lead them through the valley of the shadow of death, He has promised to lead them into the promise of rest and satisfaction. Many people miss the abundant life because they can't trust Him. They don't believe His pleasures are greater than the worlds, they don't believe He has the power to calm the storms of life, or they don't believe God is really out for their good.

One day, Jesus was sitting at dinner with the religious leaders of Israel. The meal was interrupted by a prostitute Jesus had already touched. She was so moved by the mercy shown her that she wanted to express her love for the Lord. She took the most precious heirloom she owned, an alabaster box of expensive perfumed oil. The value was nearly a year's wages. She fell at Jesus' feet, broke the box of oil, and anointed Jesus' feet.

She poured her tears onto his feet, and wiped them with her hair. It was an amazing act of love, and humility.

Did Jesus ask her to do this? Did God demand this worship? Of course not. So what drove her to do all of this without even a suggestion of Jesus, and without anyone demanding that she repay God with worship?

Jesus gives the answer. While everyone at the dinner was focused on the fact this was a sinner and woman of ill repute, the Lord asked the religious leaders a question. Who loves God more, the person who is forgiven a little, or the one who is forgiven much? Everyone answered correctly, the one who was forgiven much.

"Look at this woman," Jesus said. Then He compared her acts of love to the lack of love and worship expressed by others. They didn't believe they were forgiven of much, so they loved very little. But she, whose sins were a multitude, was forgiven of much, so she loved much.

This is why worship is forced in the church. Most do not recognize the abundance of God's grace given to them. There are three types of worshippers. Those who don't recognize that they are just as guilty as the 'bad sinners' around them, so they don't see much need for forgiveness. There are those who recognize their sins, but don't believe that all their sins are forgiven and they are completely free. Then there are those who recognize the abundance of grace, and have faith to see that all of their sins have been taken away, so they are free.

Now let's ask the same question Jesus did. "Who will love the most? Who will be compelled to pour their heart into worship? The ones who believe they are forgiven of a little, or the one who knows they are forgiven of everything?"

Your view of God's love, forgiveness, and mercy upon you will directly affect your heart of worship. The one who is loved much is the one who loves much. Worship is a response to a growing understanding of the abundance of grace poured upon us by God. The one who believes this truth will be the one who delights in worship, because they are responding to the magnitude of God's love that has removed every barrier and made them free indeed. No shame. No condemnation. It has been replaced by a heart established in grace.[9] That is when worship is born.

---

[9] Hebrews 13:9

The promise cannot be obtained outside of faith. In the same way, no problem is big enough to prevent God from bringing good into your life.

People allow condemnation back in because they look at their weaknesses, problems, and sins. Yet we are called to rest in the promise that God will transform our behavior as we keep our trust in His promise, and our eyes upon Christ.

For some, this is instant, but for others, it's a journey of faith. Sometimes we are called to trust and persevere, but the soul that turns back misses the promise that has been set aside for them to inherit. This path is not found by forcing our will into God's plan, but letting go and trusting in the coming promise. Even when you blow it, it is vital that you not allow condemnation to become your trust, but to rest in grace, knowing that you have an amazing promise. He who began a good work in you will complete it.[10]

Not every promise is realized immediately. Sometimes God calls us to trust Him when we don't see anything happening. It takes more faith to trust God with your sins than to trust God with your success.

I'm a gardener. Sometimes seeds sprout, and then have little or no growth for weeks. Some trees may go a year with no growth after being planted. From the outside, it looks like nothing is happening, but much is happening below the surface. The roots are becoming established. When the roots are strong and well established, the plant that seemed to be doing nothing for so long will suddenly burst into life.

The same is true for much of the Christian life. Your struggles may continue long after you think something should have been happening. But something IS happening, if you remain in faith. Your heart is being established in grace, and when those spiritual roots are mature, your life will blossom into amazing growth.

The reason many don't see this happen is because they give up in frustration. They are taught that if they aren't 'seeing fruit', they are failing; however, no plant has fruit year round. No plant bears fruit until it reaches a certain level of maturity.

---

[10] Philippians 1:6

Rethinking Worship

People are also taught that God is angry, disappointed, and grieved by their weaknesses and failures. So they stop trusting and stop focusing on grace. They take their eyes off of Christ, and they never allow God to establish them. The growth doesn't come because they don't trust in grace, and this causes them to turn back from the Spirit's work. Then they never experience what could only come through faith.

Joseph waited thirty years for his promise. He believed what God showed him, even when it looked impossible. He ended up getting sold into slavery by his own brothers, and then sent to prison because of someone's false accusation. He got a raw deal. Or so it seemed. How could an imprisoned slave from a foreign land be exalted to be one of the highest rulers in the country he was sold to serve? Yet it happened and he later testified, "God made me forget all my troubles."

Or what about King David? God promised that David would reign, and anointed him to be King of Israel. Yet for the next decade, King Saul persecuted him, tried to kill him, and even sent his armies to destroy David. David also ended up in a foreign country with what seemed like no hope of ever receiving what God had promised him. Then in one day, everything changed and he received what God had promised him many years earlier.

If you study the life of David and Joseph, both worshipped God in their troubles. They didn't worship God to appease Him. They worshipped in faith because they could see the promise and knew God was faithful.

You also have been promised to reign in life through Christ. Sin, circumstances, and weaknesses all try to sell you short, but those who patiently wait on the Lord will renew their strength, and then see the promise emerge out of the most impossible circumstances. Then you will look back and testify, "The Lord has made me forget all my troubles!"

In the lives of those people we have as examples in scripture, God did not demand their worship. God does not demand your worship. What God calls you to do is to open your eyes to the benefits He has provided to you. That is what inspires worship and thanksgiving. Look at **Psalm 103:2-5**

> ² Bless the LORD, O my soul, And forget not all His benefits:
> ³ Who forgives all your iniquities, Who heals all your diseases,
> ⁴ Who redeems your life from destruction, Who crowns you with lovingkindness and tender mercies,
> ⁵ Who satisfies your mouth with good *things, So that* your youth is renewed like the eagle's.

What caused David to sing with a heart of worship? He reminded himself to look at all the benefits of God. As he meditated on the goodness and love of God, he began to praise the Lord with this Psalm (or poetic song).

This is the heart of worship. When you don't feel like worshipping, it's because you have lost sight of the goodness of God toward you. You may not be experiencing all these benefits, but as you recount these promises, pray or sing them back to God, you are learning how to claim what has been given to you.

The words in this Psalm are already yours. Many promises go unclaimed because we don't feel worthy, we try to earn God's gifts, or we simply don't believe God is good or has the power to keep His word.

Here is a secret of faith. It isn't dependent upon your faith. The Bible says that God deals each of us a measure of faith. Scripture also teaches that Jesus is the Author and Finisher of our faith. Paul said that his old life was crucified with Christ, and the life he now lives, he live by the faith of Jesus Christ.

There will be times when we have trouble seeing the reality of God's promises. It is during those times when we put our confidence in the work of the Spirit through Christ. I claim the promise of faith as well as the promises given through faith. Sometimes you and I have to trust in Christ to carry us into faith, and we rely on His work of faith on our behalf. Instead of trying to make ourselves believe, which is merely a cheap substitute of human faith, we should claim the promise through the word of our testimony, and make it God's responsibility to reveal this to our natural understanding. Then rest.

It's God's job to do the work of faith, and sometimes we have to trust Him with our faith. Though our faith is weak, we still hold to the promise that when we are weak, the power of God rests upon us.[11]

Worship is born out of rest. Rest is born out of faith. Faith is when we have the eyes to see God's promises and the reality of how much He favors us. When you and I recognize His abundant benefits, it will stir thanksgiving and praise. Praise is acknowledging who God is, and thanksgiving is recognizing what God has done.

If you lack worship, instead of saying, "I must do…" stop and meditate on what God has done. Worship is always a response to God. As you are filled with grace, it overflows into worship. So if you aren't feeling grateful or worshipful, stop worrying about worship, and think upon the promises of God, and pray for God to reveal His work in your life. This is taught throughout the Bible. Now look at **Colossians 2:6-7**

> [6] As you have therefore received Christ Jesus the Lord, so walk in Him,
> [7] rooted and built up in Him and established in the faith, as you have been taught, abounding in it with thanksgiving.

Unless you are receiving, how will you abound with thanksgiving? Unless you are discovering the promise of faith, how can you worship? You are first rooted and built up in Him, and then thanksgiving will abound. As you seek Him through the word, you will be rooted and grounded. Then you will experience God's work of building you up in Christ. When you are built up in Him, it will create joy, and you will begin to overflow with thanksgiving. Let's look at a passage that teaches us how to praise. It's one of my favorite scriptures. **Ephesians 1:4-6**

> [4] just as He chose us in Him before the foundation of the world, that we should be holy and without blame before Him in love,

---

[11] 2 Corinthians 12:9

⁵ having predestined us to adoption as sons by Jesus Christ to Himself, according to the good pleasure of His will,
⁶ to the praise of the glory of His grace, by which He has made us accepted in the Beloved.

This passage destroys condemnation. You were chosen in Christ and God planned your life before you were even born. Love covers a multitude of sins, so both the sin problem is resolved, and so is any reason for you to be insecure in your Christian life. And look at the end of verse 4. You are without blame and holy because you are in His agape love!

God did this for you because it gave Him pleasure to replace your sins with His love. It is God's will for you to be a son and not an outcast. You are completely accepted because you are in the Beloved, which is Christ. When you trusted Christ, you put yourself under His works, and now you are treated as blameless as Jesus, and this produces glory to God's grace. When you understand this and know you are as beloved of a son as Jesus, it will stir a heart of praise, and you will be glorifying God's grace.

I've mentioned sons several times, so I feel the need to clarify this important truth. There are no queens in heaven. The Bible says we are all kings and priests to our God. The Bible also says we all have the inheritance as sons. Jesus made it clear that in the Kingdom of Heaven, there are no male and female roles.[12] Whether you are male or female on earth, you are counted as a son. Sons are those who inherit what belongs to the father.

In the culture when the Bible was written, females did not inherit anything. They married into someone else's inheritance. Sons inherited from their fathers. With God, all His children are treated as sons. That is why the Bible never refers to daughters when speaking of the inheritance. Daughters of God are treated as sons in the inheritance. They are not subjugated queens.

Let's look at one more passage from Psalms. Again, my goal is to show that worship is a response to the goodness of the Lord. Look at **Psalm 100:1-5**

---

[12] Matthew 22:30, Galatians 3:28

¹ Make a joyful shout to the LORD, all you lands!

¹ Make a joyful shout to the LORD, all you lands!

² Serve the LORD with gladness; Come before His presence with singing.

³ Know that the LORD, He *is* God; *It is* He *who* has made us, and not we ourselves; *We are* His people and the sheep of His pasture.

⁴ Enter into His gates with thanksgiving, *And* into His courts with praise. Be thankful to Him, *and* bless His name.

⁵ For the LORD *is* good; His mercy *is* everlasting, And His truth *endures* to all generations.

Why are the people called to worship? The Psalmist is experiencing the goodness of God, and it stirs a heart of worship. The praise and thanksgiving is a response to God making us His people. A people who have been provided for, protected, and cared for like sheep under the hand of the good shepherd. His goodness and mercy creates a heart of thankfulness.

My hope is that you rethink worship. Instead of feeling obligated to give a pretense of worship, may you learn to see the love, mercy, and goodness of God. You are God's greatly beloved. You are the disciple Jesus loves. If you feel loved by God, then you will also understand you are accepted by Him. May you see the abundant life of favor God has designed for you. May your eyes of faith teach you how to receive the abundant life, and may it cause you to overflow into praise and worship.

I pray if there is anything you take away from this book, it is that God loves you without limitations. Your success is not dependent upon your performance. Everything rests on the finished work of Christ. You don't have to become worthy. You are worthy of all God has because He has made you worthy.

Remember the words God spoke to the Apostle Peter, "What God has cleansed, you do not call unclean." You no longer have the right to condemn yourself, nor does anyone have the right to condemn you, because God has declared you clean. Let me again reiterate this passage from **1 John 4:17-19**

[17] Love has been perfected among us in this: that we may have boldness in the day of judgment; because as He is, so are we in this world.

[18] There is no fear in love; but perfect love casts out fear, because fear involves torment. But he who fears has not been made perfect in love.

[19] We love Him because He first loved us.

As Jesus is, so are you in this world. And it has nothing to do with what you have done. It's based solely upon what Christ has done and given to you.

If you fear, it is the symptom of not being made perfect in God's love. The cure is to abide in His love, which is your completeness. When you feel condemned, it's because you have lost focus on His love for you. According to the Bible, you are complete in Him.[13] Once something is complete, there is nothing left to do but rest.

Rest in the assurance of His love for you!

---

[13] Colossians 2:10

Other Recent Books by Eddie Snipes

 The Revelation of Grace. The first book in the Founded Upon Grace Series. Discover the biblical truths that explain the defeat of sin, and the unveiling of our position in Christ!

 The Spirit-Filled Life. The second book in the Founded Upon Grace Series. Discover what it means to walk in the Spirit and to live according to our inner nature, which is always receiving from the Spirit of God.

 Abounding Grace. Is there such thing as hyper-grace? What does the Bible mean by when it says that the grace of Jesus abounded over the sin that came through Adam.

More books from this author:

- It is Finished! Step out of condemnation and into the completed work of Christ.
- The Victorious Christian Life: Living in Grace and Walking in the Spirit.
- The Promise of a Sound Mind : God's plan for emotional and mental health
- Abounding Grace: Dispelling Myths and Clarifying the Biblical Message of God's Overflowing Grace
- Living in the Spirit: God's Plan for you to Thrive in the Abundant Life

Made in the USA
Middletown, DE
09 October 2018